ESCAPE FROM THE ISLAND OF OCCUPATION

Escape
From The Island
Of Occupation

Robert Plant

JOHN RITCHIE LTD
CHRISTIAN PUBLICATIONS

40 Beansburn, Kilmarnock, Scotland

ISBN-13: 978 1 909803 95 4

www.ritchiechristianmedia.co.uk

Typeset by John Ritchie Ltd., Kilmarnock
Printed by Bell & Bain Ltd., Glasgow

I dedicate this book to
The Christians who meet at
Belmont Road Gospel Hall
St Helier, Jersey
and
Green Lanes Gospel Hall
St Peter Port, Guernsey
who over many years have given me a deep love for
the Channel Islands its people, diversity and history.

Contents

Map of Jersey

CHAPTER 1

Occupation

"Jerry's restricting more of our beaches," Stan said to his wife Emily as he entered the backdoor of their Jersey granite farmhouse. Emily, a fair-haired lady in her late thirties, was absorbed in putting a patch in a pair of trousers; since the war broke out everyone had to 'make do and mend'.

She looked up at her tall, muscular husband with a blank expression on her face. "Oh, Stan, I am sorry," she apologised a few seconds later. "You're referring to the Germans, of course. I thought for a minute you were talking about our Jerry."

"I heard the news from George Le Bail that the area around Petit Bay is now out of bounds. In fact, it wouldn't surprise me if the Germans have mined the area too. They've already mined all along St. Ouen's Bay," Stan laughed sarcastically, "as if a British attack would come in at that part of the Island. Honestly, it's ridiculous! I really don't know what the Germans are getting so concerned about."

"I suppose the British forces have more on their plate than trying to reclaim the Channel Islands," Emily stated sadly, struggling to thread her needle in the dim light of the gas lamp.

"Yes, I reckon we'll just have to sit out the Occupation until the war is over."

"Maybe," Emily replied, "but I really don't like all the restrictions and new laws that the Germans are constantly bringing in. Life is really quite tiresome these days; you have to show your identity papers to go here, answer a whole bunch of questions to go there and then have to be indoors just when the Jerries say so. Why did they have to come?"

"I guess we all wonder that," Stan replied, "but they are here and so we just have to put up with it and do the best we can." He sat down and ran his fingers through his thick, brown hair.

Just then their son, Jerry, came running in. "The Germans have just sealed off Petit Bay!" he exclaimed. "Linda saw them down there and thinks that they're laying more mines! Are the Brits going to come and liberate us? The Germans must think something is afoot for them to go to all this trouble."

"I think," replied his father, leaning his large back into the chair and looking hard at his son, "that the Germans are going to go to great lengths to ensure these Islands are held under the Swastika until the end of the war. You mark my words!"

"It's not fair," Jerry said mournfully. "Soon we won't be allowed on any beaches unless the Germans give us permission."

"Yes, sadly you're right, son," his father sighed, as he bent down to undo the shoelaces on his leather boots, which had seen better days. "That's the problem with being occupied; we lose more and more freedom."

The three of them sat at the kitchen table for some time, each lost in their own thoughts of what life on the Island of Jersey had been like before the Germans had arrived: a calm, peaceful and idyllic life.

There had been a small British force on the Island but this had been moved back to England on the orders of the Prime Minister, Winston Churchill, in May 1940. Churchill had decided that it was not worth risking the lives of precious soldiers trying to defend the tiny Channel Islands. When the German army started rapidly sweeping its way through France and towards the English Channel, many of the Islanders gathered up their belongings and made their way across to England by any available passage. Those left behind waited anxiously for the inevitable invasion from the coast of France twelve miles away. They did not have long to wait!

The evening of 28th June 1940 saw German Heinkel bombers circling over the Islands. The people had rushed for cover as the planes dropped their lethal cargo of bombs around the harbour area of the town of St. Helier. Other planes swooped in, firing their machine guns at hotels and homes around the harbour front. Women had screamed and children had cried as explosion after explosion rocked the usually tranquil Island. The Islanders had no means of defending themselves as plane after plane dived out of the blue skies, bringing death and destruction. The following day an eerie quiet prevailed, only broken by the stifled sobs of those who had lost their loved ones. The horror of what had happened seemed like an unbelievable nightmare. Then from the dull grey skies leaflets dropped on the carnage demanding a full and unconditional surrender of the Islands. Jersey's Bailiff, Alexander Coutanché, appealed for calm as everyone came to terms with the awful situation in which they found themselves. This terrifying army that had overrun so much of Europe in the few short months since war had been declared, now stood poised to take over the Channel Islands of Jersey, Guernsey, Alderney, Herm and Sark, and in doing this, would bring part of British soil under the heel of the Third Reich.

The Islanders knew British help was not at hand, so as demanded by the Germans in their leaflet drop, they placed white flags outside their houses and white crosses around the Island in full surrender. Then two days after the attack the Germans landed at the airport, and were met by the Bailiff and the Attorney General.

Jerry and his parents had watched as rank after rank of German soldiers marched past them along Victoria Avenue, the seafront road. Loudspeakers had been set up in Royal Square outside the States Building, and both the Bailiff and the senior German officers had appealed to the population for calm. Yet, despite the assurances of the occupying force that everyone's safety would be solemnly guaranteed, fear and apprehension swept across the Island even quicker than the troops themselves!

For those who had chosen to stay on the Islands and not take the packed ships to England, everything had changed.

Once the Germans had arrived many orders had been issued which affected every aspect of ordinary life; from when they were allowed to go out of their homes to what time they had to be indoors, and where they could and could not go. These orders made things very difficult for the fishermen and those who worked the lobster pots. They were now restricted as to where they could fish, and even had to apply for a special licence to allow them to use their boats to fish in the waters around the Island.

The Germans were very suspicious of everyone and everything, and asked questions about almost every move that was made. Identity cards had been issued to every Islander containing their photograph and personal information. They did not dare leave home without it! All communication with England had been severed, there was no telephone contact, and no letters could reach family and friends on the mainland. However, the Germans were courteous enough, saying that this was just a temporary measure, and that restrictions on communications would be lifted as soon as England had been invaded and overrun; they seemed quite certain that would be any day now! The Islanders believed otherwise!

"Yes," thought Jerry to himself again, "everything certainly has changed." He had loved to run along the vast stretches of beach that surrounded so much of Jersey. The rock pools, sand and shallow, warm seas had been the source of hours of daily fun, especially in the holidays. Jersey had been the best place to live in the whole world!

CHAPTER 2

German Plans

As the summer of 1940 wore on, Jerry and his parents tried to continue as normally as possible with their everyday lives. Most of the Islanders had come to terms with life under occupation, and had even accepted the difficulties and new restrictions they faced daily. The majority of the German soldiers were generally nice to the Islanders, and tried to get along with them as best they could. The Islanders, however, were very cautious of any German soldier trying to be too friendly, and on occasions feelings of unease and distrust developed amongst themselves if some Islanders were seen to be acting favourably towards the soldiers.

Several months after the start of the occupation a few of the feared SS soldiers appeared on the Island. They were marked out from the regular soldiers by their totally black uniforms and the striking SS symbol on their collars, shoulders, and breast pockets. Most Islanders found these men loathsome, as they walked around with a haughty air of supremacy, making even their own German soldiers cower in their presence. The normal soldier would overlook trifling matters, but to these SS men every little law had to be upheld. Harsh punishments were handed out to any who failed to keep them.

Then the Gestapo arrived: menacing-looking men who did not wear uniforms, but instead long coats and hats, or dark glasses. They were the ones to be feared the most; spies who hauled alleged troublemakers down to their formidable headquarters in Havre Des Pas for the harshest of questionings.

Jerry first came across the Gestapo when he was out with

Linda one afternoon. Linda, a very pretty brunette, lived on the farm next to Jerry's. She was a good friend to Jerry and quite a tomboy who would take on any challenge. There were certainly no boys as good at climbing trees as she was. Jerry had seen her effortlessly climb one of the tall pine trees that overlooked the northern end of St. Ouen's Bay one day after school when Jimmy Clement dared her to. Jimmy was certain that Linda's attempt would end in a sure defeat for her, but on the contrary, accomplishing this she gained respect from all her peers. After this nobody dared to question her ability to do anything. She would outrun most boys on school sports day, not just in sprinting, but over a much longer distance as well. However, not only was Linda athletic, she was clever too.

From the time that the Germans had arrived on the Island, Linda had decided to try to learn their language. "Not," she had said, "to make friends with them or impress them, but so that I can understand what they say, then hopefully pick up information that we are not supposed to know!" So, more or less from the day the Occupation began, Linda had sought, with the aid of an old German dictionary she had discovered in the attic, to string together a few phrases. She would try these out whenever she came across a German soldier.

Linda had also learnt how to take a tractor's engine apart and put it back together again. Often Jerry had walked across the fields adjoining their two farms to find Linda wearing a checked shirt, overalls several sizes too big, sleeves rolled up and arms covered in grease as she worked on the carburettor or oil sump of the farm tractor. She had even tried to service the family car, but had been banned from that after she had removed the gearbox and been unable to put it back again! Still, for a girl of thirteen, Jerry decided that she was almost as good, if not better, than two boys the same age.

Linda and Jerry had decided that afternoon to walk down the main road from their homes towards the wide sandy expanse of St. Aubin's Bay, straddled by Elizabeth Castle to the east and St. Aubin's Fort to the west. As they neared the inner coast road an open topped German staff car swerved hard around the corner and screeched to a halt. A tall, lean man, clean-shaven, with fair hair and protruding jaw, was sitting in the back seat just behind the driver. He shouted something in German in a loud and bad-tempered manner to the driver who immediately leapt out of his seat to let his passenger out. The tall man then strode over to where Jerry and Linda were standing and in very good English said, "Your papers!"

Both Jerry and Linda were a bit taken aback and Jerry stammered in a rather weak and pathetic voice. "P-p-pardon?"

"Your papers!" the man demanded again. "Your identity papers," he snapped, "I want to see them!"

Linda pulled out her identity card from her shirt pocket and handed it to the man who read it, paying particular attention to the photograph on it. He handed it back. Jerry's rather tatty card was quickly snatched from him and the stern faced man took what seemed to be a lifetime to scan his eyes over it.

"What are you doing?" he growled at them.

"We were j-j-j-just going down to the front to see the sea," stammered Jerry.

"Is there a law against that?" asked Linda confidently.

"Hum," he replied brusquely. "Not yet, but you be very careful." The man turned on his heels and strode irately back to the car.

Both Jerry and Linda breathed a long sigh of relief as he climbed into the back. They watched as the driver started the engine and drove off in the direction of St. Lawrence Church.

"Phew," said Jerry. "I don't know about you, but I was quaking in my boots."

"Yes," agreed Linda. "He must have been from the Gestapo and was just trying to frighten us."

"Well, he did that all right!" replied Jerry. "Come on, let's get down to the seafront."

Jerry and Linda arrived at the seafront and stood for a while enjoying the sea breeze, and admiring the wide expanse of the bay. As they looked further out towards the water's edge, they could see dozens of German soldiers busily working along the beach.

A local man, with a pipe dangling from the side of his mouth, stood a few yards from the two friends. "Hum, must think that the Allies are going to land here with tanks and big guns," said the man, to no one in particular.

"What do you mean?" Linda asked the stranger.

"Well, the Germans have captured the only part of the British Isles they are likely to capture, and now they are terrified that Mr Churchill will try to take the Islands back by force. As if old Winston hasn't enough to worry about just now."

"Hey," Jerry butted in, "my dad thinks like that too...err..." He stopped as if unsure as to what he had just said. "At least the bit about them trying to attack the Island; he says it won't happen."

"No, it won't, young'un," the old man replied, knocking his pipe on the side of the wall that they were looking over. "Complete waste of time all this effort along here to stop the Allies landing on this beach," he continued, motioning to where the soldiers were working.

"Is that what it is?" Linda asked, looking out across the beach. "To stop anyone landing on the beach?"

"Ah, lass, it is that. That's mines they are laying to stop anyone that lands there getting any nearer." The old man looked at the two youngsters as if he had just noticed them for the first time. "No, they won't invade here, that's why Britain will win this war and Germany will lose. The Germans are too fussy about little matters whilst the British get on with the fighting and winning. You wait and see!" He turned and looked again at them, "Great shame for you two, having to grow up in such days under German rule. I've had my good times, let's hope and pray that you will be given the same chances." He paused. "I know Germany will lose, but I think the war will be a long and hard one." With that, he walked sadly away, shaking his head.

Jerry and Linda continued to watch the Germans carrying on their work in the distance a little longer, and then turned to walk back up the valley towards their homes.

"You know," said Jerry, "I think that old man is right, the Germans will lose the war eventually, but what I'd give to be able to join in and get them off this Island so that we could all live in peace again."

"Me too," joined in Linda eagerly. "If only there was something we could do to get rid of them."

"Well, we could pray," Jerry added, a sudden eagerness rising in his voice.

"Pray!" Linda answered in surprise.

"Yes, pray," Jerry repeated. "That old man said we should hope and pray. My Uncle Fred believes in God and prays all the time, and at least praying is doing something."

Linda looked unimpressed by Jerry's idea and added as they turned into the driveway that led to Jerry's house, "Well, I think it needs a bit more than that."

CHAPTER 3

The Search

"The Germans have issued an order requesting that all guns be handed in," Stan said rather sombrely that evening, as he placed the copy of the Jersey Evening Post that he had just been reading on the table. "They have given all the Islanders forty-eight hours to take any weapons they have down to headquarters in St. Helier."

"Well," said Emily, "we have two shotguns so let's hand one over and hide the other. Then I bet they'll want our radios soon. I don't think I could bear not being able to find out what is going on around the world from the BBC in London."

"Too right," replied Stan. "The Germans will never tell us the truth if the British win a victory against them; all they will tell us is how well the war is progressing for the Third Reich. Anyway, I agree that we should keep one of the guns, just in case."

"But," said Jerry with an anxious expression on his face, "what will happen if the Germans find the gun?"

"They won't," his dad assured him, placing his hand on Jerry's shoulder. "Trust me; I know just the place to hide it!"

The next day, Jerry and his father walked the three miles from their home to the town to hand in one of their two guns. Jerry watched nervously as his father handed over the gun along with a few cartridges. The German soldier wrote down his father's name and address, and the make and type of the gun he had brought in. Many others were queuing in line, carrying various types and sizes of guns or other weapons. A German sentry stood outside, keeping a close eye on the queue, with his own gun slung loosely across his shoulder.

Jerry then heard the German ask his father in perfect English, "Is this the only weapon you have in the house, Mr Le Godel?"

Jerry took a sharp intake of breath, then heard his father say, "Yes, indeed. I have no other weapon in our house."

"Very good," said the German as he handed the gun carefully to an assistant behind him. "Next, please."

Jerry and his father went outside and started to walk along the main street. As they passed by the various shops on their way home, they noticed some new signs that the Germans were displaying in the shop windows. Jerry's dad suddenly stopped stone dead; he was staring at one new addition that had been stuck to the glass of one shop. In large, black letters the words 'Jewish Undertaking' were written in both German and English, above the sign was the Star of David.

"Oh dear," whispered Stan under his breath. "So it is true after all."

"What's true?" asked Jerry.

"That the German army are persecuting the Jews," replied his father, as they continued walking up the cobbled street. "That shop belongs to a Jewish family, and I have been told that the German army, on Hitler's orders, have been making Jews in Europe wear the Star of David, which is sort of their national emblem. That means that whenever you see a person in the street wearing a star you will immediately know that he or she is a Jew." Then looking down on his son, he added, "It's a sad business."

"Dad," asked Jerry, as they walked up Queen's Road, "why did you lie to that German about our other gun? You have always told me that I have to be truthful."

"That's right," replied his father, "but you see, son, we do not actually have another gun in the house. I have hidden it in the barn, in a box I made especially for it. They won't find it there. We might need it in the future to defend ourselves, so it is important we hold onto it."

Jerry and his father walked on up the hill and then turned left to head across the Island to the Parish of St. Lawrence where they lived. For the first time, Jerry was beginning to understand something of the seriousness of the occupation and also what could happen to them if the Germans found the gun his dad had so carefully hidden.

One sunny Thursday afternoon, about a month later, the Germans came calling. Jerry heard a loud knock on the front door and ran to open it, expecting to see Linda standing in the doorway. As he swung open the door, his heart missed a beat. He found himself looking up into the faces of three German soldiers.

"Are your parents at home?" one of them drawled slowly as he sought to find the right English words to use.

"Yes...yes...my, my, my mother is baking bread in the kitchen," Jerry managed to stammer out, his throat suddenly feeling very dry and his heart pounding. The first man, who was obviously more senior, pushed past Jerry and walked down the hallway towards the kitchen at the back of the house. Just then Emily appeared, her arms white with flour.

"Good afternoon, madam," said the German officer. "This is just a routine inspection of your premises; hopefully we will not be too long."

"Oh, but what are you hoping to find?" asked Emily, trying to be calm.

"Nothing, we trust, unless you are trying to tell me that you have illegal goods in your possession," replied the officer. "It will be much better for you to own up now and hand them over, rather than for my men to find them, as they most certainly will!"

"Carry on, you have a job to do," Stan boomed, as his large frame appeared in the open doorway of the house.

"Good," said the officer. "Then you will not mind if we search your premises?"

With that, he directed the two men with him up the stairs. Once they were out of sight, Stan put his arm around Emily. She tried to keep the tears from her eyes and the fear from her face. They heard the men upstairs as their jackboots made heavy clanking noises on the wooden floors. Eventually they came back down into the front room of the house. The officer immediately noticed the open fireplace and instructed one of the men to examine the chimney above it. The soldier got down on all fours and shone a torch into the darkness above the cold hearth. Furniture was moved around, and floors and walls prodded and tapped as the men searched for any type of hiding place. Having examined every cupboard and drawer in the kitchen, the men moved out into the courtyard and across to the barn, followed by both Stan and Jerry.

As soon as they entered the barn, Jerry noticed that his father had penned three cows into one corner - the corner under which Jerry guessed the shotgun was hidden. The German soldiers contented themselves with moving various bales of hay around as they searched for any tell-tale signs of a hiding place. Eventually, having looked casually at the cows in their pen, they walked over to them and the officer ordered the two soldiers to enter the pen. The two looked at each other and then their commanding officer.

"They are all tame," Stan offered with a chuckle.

One of the soldiers moved the nearest wooden fencing panel which was tied with thin rope aside and cautiously entered the pen, nudging the cows around as he searched below the straw that was scattered at the cows' feet. He kicked the straw around the pen and stamped his feet, listening for any hollow sounds that might suggest a secret hiding place. He moved around carefully, trying to avoid the cowpats that lay on the floor. Once he was satisfied, he came out of the enclosure, and Jerry and his father watched with some amusement as the soldier tried to replace the wooden fence and tie it securely with the rope, whilst at the same time the cows, seeing a possible escape route, tried to push the wooden gate open. The soldier, who by now was perspiring heavily, struggled valiantly to tie the rope and keep the cows in the pen. At last he succeeded and all of them came out of the barn. The soldier who had entered the cow pen, despite his best efforts, had not been too successful in avoiding the cowpats and stood furiously wiping cow dung off his jackboots onto the grass.

The officer spoke to Stan, "Sorry to have disturbed you and your family, Mr Le Godel, but we just have to carry out this sort of search every now and again."

"Thank you," said Stan hoarsely, "I understand." The three soldiers climbed into their car, and turning it round, headed down the track that led from the farm to the road.

"That was too close for comfort!" Emily exclaimed.

"Yes," said Stan, "it's a good job I had those three cows with me in the barn or the Germans may have found that gun. I saw them approaching, which gave me just enough time to usher the cows into that corner and make the pen look like the real thing."

"Great stuff!" said Jerry excitedly, as he applauded his father's quick thinking. "You're the best!"

CHAPTER 4

Hitler's Coming!

"Hey," Linda called to Jerry across the fields. "Have you heard the news?"

"What news?" enquired Jerry inquisitively.

"Hitler's coming to the Island! My dad has just heard about it from a German soldier!"

"What, you mean Adolf Hitler?" gasped Jerry. "Hitler's coming to Jersey?! Don't be silly! He can't be!"

"Well, that's what my dad has heard," protested his friend, as she climbed over a gate that separated the fields between their two farms, and dropped down into the same field as Jerry. "Apparently he wants to use his visit as a propaganda exercise, you know the sort of thing, 'German Chancellor standing on British soil'."

"Yeah," said Jerry thoughtfully, "I can see his thinking; that would make great publicity for him, wouldn't it?"

The two friends looked at each other thoughtfully for some time without saying a word. Eventually Linda spoke, putting into words what they were both thinking. "Wouldn't it be great if we could stop him from coming?"

"It would," replied Jerry thoughtfully. "If only there was a way to either stop him, or even better, get rid of him!"

"Yes, get rid of him!" breathed out Linda in a low whisper. "Get rid of him," she repeated. The two stood and stared at each other open-mouthed at the ridiculous idea they had suggested.

"Wow! Just think what would happen if he was killed," said Jerry. "The war would be over!"

"But," interjected Linda, rousing from her faraway thinking, "who could do it, and how could it be done?"

"I don't know," responded Jerry, "but I bet Dad will have some ideas. Let's go and ask him."

"Dad, Dad!" called Jerry excitedly as he and Linda ran along the lane around the side of the farm. His father ambled out of the barn with his sleeves rolled up and oil stains on his hands.

"What's all the fuss about?" he asked, as he watched the two racing towards him.

"A German soldier has told Linda's dad that he's heard that Hitler's coming to Jersey, so what do you think we should do about it?" Jerry blurted out, without pausing for breath.

"Whoa, now," said Stan to the two excited teenagers. "Who's told Linda's dad?"

"A German soldier," repeated Jerry in an exasperated voice, appalled at his dad's lack of understanding of the importance of the piece of news. "Do you not see, Dad, this will be our chance to get him!"

"To get who?" asked his father, as he looked at the two youngsters in a rather bemused manner.

"Hitler, of course," Linda blurted. "He is coming to the Island soon and we have to try and get him whilst he's here."

"Just hang on a minute," said Jerry's father, holding up a hand and stopping the two almost in mid-sentence. "Let's calm down. Come on, we'll go inside and talk in a more rational manner over a warm drink."

"Well, now, that is interesting," mused Emily as she listened to their extraordinary news. She poured a cup of tea from the teapot as she continued, "But what chance have the Jersey people got of actually getting near Hitler when he does come? I don't think any at all; he will be so heavily defended that even the seagulls won't be able to land on Jersey the day he comes!"

"Yes, but we have got to do something," replied Jerry, as he took a homemade bun from a tin. "This may be the best chance anyone has of bumping old Adolf off, whilst he's away from the safety of Germany!"

His father, who had been sitting quietly, listening intently to the conversation, suddenly joined in, "What we need to do is to get news of when he is coming to the Allies in England, so that they can be ready to intercept him when he arrives. Obviously he will have to come either by air or sea, and that would be when he would be most vulnerable."

"I think first you need to ensure that this news is really true, and not just a tall story that some bored German soldier has invented to cause a stir and a little excitement among the troops here in Jersey," suggested Emily.

The next couple of days both Jerry and Linda tried to find out if what they had heard was actually true. It was very hard not being able to ask direct questions of the many soldiers that they saw every day on their way to and from school, or even to ask friends at school or older people they trusted. They were worried that, if they did, word might get back to the Gestapo that they were asking too many questions and then they could be arrested by those fearful and hated men.

About a week after hearing the news, they were making their way across the fields and down various lanes to school, when they came upon a rather comical-looking German corporal who seemed much too old to be in the army. He was leaning on a wooden fence and apparently speaking to a herd of Jersey cows on the other side! As he heard the children approaching, he stood bolt upright and looked at them, his face bright red with embarrassment.

"Guten morgen!" he said in German. "I...used to be...cattle farmer...in Bavaria but then come...war," he continued in broken English. He stopped and sighed as he remembered his home. The two youngsters noticed a tear well up in his eye and start to roll down his cheek. "We not...all bad," he said, after wiping his face with the back of his hand. He looked anxiously around before adding, "Many of us...not like Hitler! Ja?"

Quick as a flash, Linda butted in, "But I thought Hitler was coming here to this Island, to Jersey. We heard he was coming soon."

"Ja," replied the soldier, "so say the higher…auth…auth… how you say?"

"Authority," Jerry offered, as the German struggled to find the right pronunciation.

"Wow," said Linda, "to think that Hitler is really going to come here, to our Island! That will be something. Do you know when?" she asked their newfound friend.

"I not…sure, but hear it could…be next week," he answered. "Hitler make no plans long term in case someone not like him."

"Hum!" snorted Jerry. "I can understand that."

"Well, we must hurry now or we'll be late for school," said Linda. "Nice to meet you. Goodbye."

"Auf Wiedersehen," called the corporal, as they sped away along the lane, taking the right-hand fork that led to their school.

The two friends were so excited they could hardly concentrate on their lessons. To think that the German Chancellor was planning to visit the Island next week! They could hardly wait to tell the news back home.

CHAPTER 5

Who Will Go?

"Well, I have heard some rumours too," said Emily, as she passed the bowl of Jersey Royal potatoes across the table to her husband. "I met Mrs Le Sueur in the market and she has heard that the Germans are tightening up security at the airport, and that another two infantry divisions are due on the Island in the next few days, but only for a limited time. So it looks like your initial reports are right."

"If only we could get word over to England," said her husband. "As I said before, that would be when old Adolf would be at his most vulnerable flying across to here. Just imagine if the RAF could shoot his plane down!"

"Hey, that's what Linda and I had thought," cut in Jerry excitedly. "Well," he corrected himself, "not exactly that, shooting down his plane, I mean, but to do him in while he is here in Jersey, and Linda and I have been making plans as to how to do it."

"Well, you just be careful with your plans," scolded his father. "If the feldgendarmerie get to hear about them you will be in trouble, and more trouble than you can cope with." He turned to look out of the window and a serious frown came upon his tanned face. "No, what is needed is not an assassination in Jersey as no one will get near him. What would be best is for him either never to get here at all, or never to get back. The problem is," he added thoughtfully, "how can we contact the Allies and let them know what little information we have about his proposed visit."

They were all silent as they thought about the importance of their discussion. Someone had to find a way of getting a message from Jersey to England, and it had to be done fast for there to be any chance at all of using this visit to get rid of the German leader and ending the dreadful war.

Jerry lay awake for much of the night wondering how anyone could get a message back to England with such important information. He realised perhaps for the first time since the Island's invasion just how cut off they were from England and the rest of the world. "How can it be done?" Jerry thought over and over again, as he tossed and turned beneath the blankets of his bed. "And, if it can be done, who should go and do it?" Eventually he drifted into a restless sleep, only to awake early the next morning still trying to think of a way of getting a message to England.

He was up and dressed without the usual calls from his mother, and made his way down into the kitchen. There he found his father already conversing with his mother across the kitchen table.

"You see, Emily, if this information really is true then we must find a way to let those in England know, so that they can be ready to get Hitler when he is at his most vulnerable." His tone was firm and serious as he gazed towards his wife who was sitting opposite him wiping a glass jug with a tea towel. "If I can get hold of a small boat I might be able to get it off the Island around the top of St. Ouen's Bay and make my way up towards the Isle of Wight. Of course I will need fuel, and an engine reliable enough to get me across the English Channel."

"But Dad," said Jerry, in a voice that shook with both fear and worry, "you can't go! You must not go; surely someone else can go instead of you!"

"That may be so," replied his father kindly. "However, someone must go, and at the moment I am volunteering!"

CHAPTER 6

The Plan

Jerry was filled with fear and a little bit of excitement as he left for school that day. He knew that what his father was thinking of doing was incredibly dangerous. Not only would he have to travel about a hundred miles across the English Channel in a small boat, but he also ran the risk of either being captured by the occupying German forces on the Island before he left, or by the German Navy once he was out at sea. Even if he did get away, Jerry knew how temperamental and difficult the little outboard motors could be, and should the motor fail and the tides be running the wrong way, his father could end up drifting right out into the Atlantic Ocean.

However, he could hardly wait to tell Linda of his father's daring plan.

When Linda heard the plan she spoke with a maturity and confidence beyond her young age. "Your father would never make it," she declared to a stunned Jerry. "He would not get off the Island, well at least not from the top of St. Ouen's. It's far too heavily fortified. No, the only way to get safely off the Island is to leave from the bottom of the north coast cliffs. Those cliffs cannot be mined except for maybe some of the gullies, so they don't pay too much attention to that area, although I bet it won't stay that way for long as the Germans are mining everywhere else."

Jerry looked at her long and hard. "Why are you so certain that my dad will not make it?" he questioned.

"Look," replied Linda in an almost exasperated voice, "I have looked over just about every part of this Island since the Germans arrived, both during the day and at night after curfew, and I know that the only safe way off this Island is by the north coast cliffs."

"At night!" Jerry gasped. "You have been walking around this Island in the dark after curfew?! Why, you could have been killed!"

"I guess you are right," Linda replied, "but at least I know where all the main guards are situated and which areas are safe to go to and which are not. I have made plans and diagrams as well in the hope that someday I can get them across to England. They may be helpful if the British ever decide to invade the Island."

Jerry was still reeling at the news of his friend's night-time exploits when she went on to say, "You know, I believe that you and I have a much better chance than your father has of making it across to England."

"Why do you say that?" asked Jerry, in an unbelieving tone.

"Because," replied Linda, "I know the best route off the north coast, and we are so young our absence may not be as noticeable, especially in the coming school holidays. I also know about engines, so I reckon I should be able to fix the motor on the boat just as well as your dad should anything go wrong with it." Linda threw her head back with a slightly nervous laugh. "So, what do you think?"

"Um, and I suppose with school holidays starting next week we might just get away with it." Jerry stood there in silence for a while staring out of the small school window that overlooked the cobbled playground and the side of a house at the far end. "Well," he said thoughtfully, "I would be much happier going rather than allowing Dad to go and me waiting here with Mum not knowing what had happened to him. But then what about our parents; what will they say? They certainly won't want to let us go!"

"No! No! NO!" Jerry's father's voice echoed through the house as he made his feelings clear to his son later on that night. "There is no way that you are going to make the trip. Absolutely not!" Although his voice was determined, his manner was kindly as he looked at his son. "I will go, but firstly we need to find out as much as we can about the plans that are in place for Hitler's visit. It's no good anyone risking their lives unnecessarily. The British will need as much information about his visit as possible. We can't go all that way just to pass on a bit of hearsay or rumour. That would be as good as useless to the Allies; they will need firm facts to go on." He looked at his wife across the table and sighed deeply.

"What a job for anyone to have to undertake," said Emily. "I wish this war had never happened. Who would have thought there would be a second world war? Everyone thought the last war was the war to end all wars. Why, oh why, did someone like Hitler have to be born?" she complained.

Next day was Saturday, and despite what Jerry's father had said, Jerry and Linda decided to explore as much as they could of the cliffs on the north of the Island, with the idea of taking a boat themselves and getting the information to England. This area was not patrolled as frequently as some of the beaches due to the high cliffs that towered some three hundred feet above sea level. The cliffs were home to a variety of nesting birds and other wildlife which both youngsters had enjoyed watching in the idyllic days before the occupation. Looking due north on a clear day from the top of these cliffs, the smaller Island of Alderney could be seen, a turn of the head to the west brought Guernsey into sight and by looking east, the French coast came into view. On this beautiful summer's day the friends were lost in their own worlds, the warm sun beating down upon them as they rambled across the various fields and through the woods that occasionally covered the cliff tops, in their search for a suitable area from which to make their escape.

"It's impossible," sighed Jerry after several hours of exploration and the occasional dodging of a German guard. "You could never get a boat down these cliffs without it being damaged, and the oil and diesel would spill on the way down making it useless at the bottom."

"No it wouldn't," replied Linda firmly. "We would take the

engine down separately and then attach it to the boat when we are at the bottom. In fact, I was thinking that maybe we could hide a store at the bottom of the cliffs before we go, so that it does not all have to be taken down at one time, you know - engine, jerry cans, food and the like."

"You mean make several trips instead of just one?" enquired Jerry rather apprehensively.

"Yes," came back Linda's firm reply. "The more we can get down as close to the sea as possible, the less we have to take the night we leave, and the more chance we will have of getting away."

"But what if the Jerries see us or catch us?" argued her friend.

"Well, we will just have to make sure they don't, won't we?" Linda's confidence in the ability of the two to succeed was undaunted by Jerry's apparent concerns at the difficulties that would be encountered in climbing up and down a three hundred foot cliff, carrying the various heavy items of gear they would need.

After much discussion, both felt that the area around the blowhole, known as 'Devil's Hole', would be the most suitable. There they felt sure that there would be suitable crevasses and ledges near the bottom to hide the various items required for the journey. The next thing they would need to do would be to find a way to descend the cliffs safely. Despite her apparent confidence, Linda was well aware of the dangers of lowering themselves down to the rocks on the shore and at the same time avoiding detection by the German patrols operating in that area.

Once back at Linda's farm, she raced into an old barn and swung herself up onto a ledge about twelve feet from the ground by means of the hay bales and a stepladder.

"I am sure we will need this to get down that cliff," Linda said as she unhooked an old dusty rope and threw it down in front of Jerry. Jerry took a step back as the brown coils landed heavily at his feet. "I just hope that it's long enough," she added. "We will have to measure it, so hang on a minute," she called, as she jumped down and went into another stone outbuilding before reappearing with a wooden ruler that unfolded to measure a yard. "Right," she stated, "I have Dad's old yardstick here so we can measure this rope with it." She opened the wooden ruler out at its hinges and then swung the rest around to make a long, straight stick. "Remember learning this in school?" she asked with a smile on her face. "Three feet make a yard and this stick is three feet long, so that means we need one hundred or more lengths of this, to make sure we have enough rope. It's going to take time so let's get started."

CHAPTER 7

Dodging Danger

It took the pair a lot longer than they thought it would to measure out the length of rope. At the end of their efforts both were intensely disappointed to discover that the rope only stretched to about one hundred and seventy-five feet. They needed another one hundred and twenty-five feet, and that was not allowing for them tying one end of the rope to a tree and the other end around themselves before lowering themselves down the cliff face. Both sat on the barn floor looking at each other despondently.

"Well," said Jerry, suddenly coming to life, "there is just one thing for us to do and that is to get hold of either another rope that is longer than this one, or one that we can tie to this one to make it long enough, and I think I know just the place to get it."

"Where?" asked Linda, pulling herself to her feet and looking enquiringly at Jerry.

"I remember once," he went on, "walking past a lock-up garage near La Colomberie in town. The door of the garage was open and I happened to stop and look in, and inside were two German soldiers taking various items off the shelves, and amongst an assortment of uniforms and other bits and pieces I am sure I remember seeing several lengths of rope."

"But you can't just walk in there and take what you like, you know; it will be locked and guarded."

"Locked, yes; guarded, no," retorted Jerry, with a feeling of pleasure that this time he knew more than Linda. "The Jerries don't guard their store rooms, they just keep them locked, so it would just be a case of dodging their patrols and forcing the lock so that we could get in, then we take what we want, replace the lock as best we can, and get away. I think it would be best done at night under cover of darkness and after the curfew."

"Well, then," said Linda in a rather low and hoarse voice, "what's stopping us going tonight?"

Jerry listened as the old grandfather clock, which had been in his family for several generations, chimed out the midnight hour. He cautiously climbed out of bed and slipped on the darkest pair of trousers that he had, as well as a thick, dark jersey. He took an old pair of knitted socks and stuffed them into his pocket. He had once watched an old film at the cinema where socks were put over shoes to stop them from making a noise on the streets during an escape in the First World War. Then quietly he unlatched his bedroom door and crept down the stairs to the hallway, every creak and squeak making his hair stand on end. He had not dared to tell his parents what they were planning! Jerry felt a real sense of elation as he finally stepped outside and softly closed the front door behind him. That was the first stage over. The next stage was to get to St. Helier without being caught.

Jerry had arranged to meet Linda next to a tree between their two farms; they then planned to travel as far as possible across fields in order to avoid any German soldiers that might be patrolling the roads. This meant taking a much longer route than they would normally use to go into town.

They met up as planned, both full of a mixture of trepidation and excitement at the adventure that lay before them. Cautiously they crossed the fields and occasional roads as they edged closer to the town. Once at the top of La Pouquelaye they took their extra pairs of socks out of their pockets and pulled them over their shoes. Ever so cautiously they edged through the town. Every nerve was strained and every sense alert as they picked their way through the deserted and darkened streets. Suddenly they heard the unmistakable sound of German jackboots stomping along the road towards them. Quickly they dived down the stone steps of one of the townhouses and squatted in the doorway of the basement. Their hearts were racing as two German soldiers on patrol walked past, conversing in their own hard, guttural language. The two of them sheltered there for a long time trying to steady their nerves, until they felt sure that no other German soldiers were following on behind.

Eventually they emerged from their hiding place and headed for the lock-up garage. They rounded the corner at the top of La Colomberie and then ducked in and out of various doorways until they were at last standing outside the garage door. Linda produced a large, rusty, pointed, iron crowbar that she had been carrying strapped to her body, and placed the point into the loop of the padlock.

"Where did you get that from?" Jerry whispered in amazement.

"I tied it to myself and hid it under my jersey," Linda replied.

They both pushed the bar hard in an effort to break the padlock. Suddenly the point of the crowbar slipped out of the loop and Jerry and Linda crashed into the garage door as they fell to the ground, making a great commotion. They picked themselves up as quickly as possible and ran round the nearest corner and into a recessed doorway. There they waited, their hearts beating wildly, expecting someone to come at any minute to investigate the noise. One minute passed, then two, then three and then five. Eventually ten minutes passed, and still they heard no sounds from the garage. They inched cautiously along the side of the street and peered round the corner towards the lock-up. There was no one about. Edging nearer to the garage again, they noticed that in their mad flight they had left the iron bar lying at the foot of the door. Quickly they picked up the crowbar and this time, standing each side of the lock, they inserted the bar and pushed hard downward. They strained with all their might but the lock just would not give.

"Just a minute," said Jerry looking at the clasp hinge into which the lock fitted. "We are trying to break the wrong part. We need to force this clasp as it's only screwed into the wood and it will give way far more easily than that old lock!"

Linda agreed and immediately placed the point down between the lock and one side of the garage door. Jerry pushed hard. The door was so tightly closed he could only force the point down a little way. Linda kept a sharp lookout whilst Jerry attempted to force the lock. Eventually the bar moved a little further down behind the lock. Once he was satisfied that he had pushed the bar down far enough, he pulled on it with all his might. There was a loud cracking sound as the screws in the wooden door of the garage gave way. Moving quickly, Jerry replaced the bar further down the back of the lock and gave it another almighty pull. There was another loud crack as the final screws came loose from the wood and released the door. The two carefully opened the door and cautiously stepped inside the dark interior. With no windows in the garage, the only light was that from the moon that came through a small skylight in the roof. After a few minutes they felt confident enough to proceed further into the garage, which was about fifteen feet long and eight to ten feet wide.

"I wouldn't like to park a car in here," whispered Jerry. "You'd hardly be able to open the doors."

"Never mind parking cars," Linda answered, "we are here to find some rope."

Wooden shelving ran along both sides of the garage filled with an assortment of items that the two friends could not see, but could only feel with their hands. They groped their way along the various heights of shelves feeling for the rope that they desperately needed for their planned escape.

Eventually Linda whispered through the darkness, "Hey! I've found one. I've found a rope!"

Slowly Jerry moved in the direction of Linda's whispered call. He felt along the shelves with his hands and lifted a rough, plaited length of one inch hemp rope. "Yes," he breathed, "this is what we need." He lifted the coil of rope down off the shelf and hoisted it onto his shoulder.

"Wow!" he gasped. "I had no idea it could be so heavy."

"Just a minute," Linda said to him. "It looks awfully thin. Are you sure that it will hold us on those cliffs?"

"It better had," stammered Jerry as he shifted the heavy coil of rope into a slightly more comfortable position on his shoulder.

The two friends cautiously opened the garage door and looked around. All was still and silent. Jerry moved out first and tiptoed across the road and into a darkened doorway. Linda followed after attempting to straighten the lock to make it less obvious that it had been tampered with. Then it was a cat and mouse dash through the shadowy streets of St. Helier. They made it safely to the edge of the town, but by this time Jerry was really feeling the weight of the rope over his shoulder.

"Let me carry it a bit," whispered Linda as they took a well-earned rest behind a hedge.

"You'll never be able to manage it," scoffed Jerry, forgetting for a moment how capable Linda was.

"Of course I will," retorted Linda. "I have almost lifted Dad's tractor engine out by myself before now, as you well know! Go on; let me take it for a bit. Here, you carry the crowbar."

Reluctantly Jerry agreed and let the rope drop from his aching shoulder. Linda took it up and almost effortlessly threw it up and onto her own shoulder.

It was a hard climb back to their farmhouses. The weight of the rope, although shared between them, was certainly very taxing as they trudged wearily back across the fields towards home.

At last they arrived back safely at their original meeting place, and after Jerry had agreed to take responsibility for the rope they parted and went their ways to their own farmhouses. Exhausted, Jerry threw the rope behind the bags of animal feed in their barn and crept back up the stairs and into his bedroom. As he removed his clothes and slipped back into his pyjamas he realised he was trembling from head to toe with the strain of the escapade. If he could only have seen across into the neighbouring farmhouse he would have known that Linda was shaking equally as much!

CHAPTER 8

The Parents

The next day the two friends walked the familiar road to school. The fear and excitement was still fresh in their minds, but today as they trudged wearily along, the road seemed much longer than usual.

"What we need next," said Linda all of a sudden, "is an outboard motor, or better still, two motors and a small boat."

"What do we need two motors for?" asked Jerry, looking puzzled.

"In case one breaks down, silly," she answered. "Come on, or we'll be late for school."

School seemed to drag more than usual that day; neither child wanted to be wasting time in school when they could be getting ready for their great escapade. They felt the destiny of the war was in their hands.

That day the children were informed that an order from the Island Commandant had been given that German was to be taught in all the schools, commencing after the summer holidays.

Linda was good at languages. "In fact," thought Jerry, as the news was announced, "Linda is good at everything, and she already knows some German." However, neither of them had any desire to spend time learning German in school just because their invaders demanded it.

At the end of the school day they headed home, once again deep in conversation.

"You know, Linda, my Uncle Fred has a small boat he used to go fishing in," confided Jerry. "I have been in it with him on a few occasions both fishing and to empty some lobster pots which he had out at St. Catherine's. I wonder if we would be able to borrow his boat and motor." Jerry paused and thought carefully, "The problem is, we'd have to let our folks know what we are doing...and you know what my father's reaction was the first time I mentioned it."

Linda made a long thinking sound, "Ummmmm, you know, I think we really do need to let our parents in on what we want to do." Jerry fell silent as Linda continued, "You see, I think we will need their help in getting the boat and the supplies down that cliff. I don't think we will reach the bottom safely without their involvement."

"But," said Jerry after a long pause, "what if our parents stop us altogether?"

"Do you remember you mentioned something about prayer the other day?" Linda asked quizzically.

"Yes, I do," Jerry answered.

"Well, if there is a God then we need Him to answer this prayer more than any, that our parents understand our point of view and are willing to let us go."

"I think you're right, it's definitely worth a try. My dad believes in God but not the same way as Uncle Fred. That's why Dad always insists on me telling the truth. Anyway, let's pray tonight and then ask our parents tomorrow."

"Okay, I agree," replied Linda, not really believing it would make any difference.

"Please, dear God, Linda and I need Your help real bad," Jerry prayed that night. "You see, Adolf Hitler is coming to the Island and he's a real bad man and we need to let folks in England know that he's coming, so they can kill him and stop this awful war. And," he continued, "I also think, God, that only Linda and me can make it down those cliffs and over to England to warn them, so please let our mums and dads be helpful and please make them let us go. Amen!" Jerry lost count how many times through that long, dark night he prayed that prayer as he drifted in and out of a fitful sleep.

The next morning, even before he was dressed, Jerry raced

excitedly downstairs for breakfast to find that his parents were not even up yet! Reluctantly he returned to his bedroom and got dressed. This time when he ventured downstairs his father was sitting at the table eating a slice of toast.

"Dad," ventured Jerry, in a rather wary manner, "I have been thinking about how you are going to get across to England to warn them about Hitler's visit."

His father stopped chewing on his toast and looked up at his son, "Oh you have, have you?"

"Well yes, but not just me, Linda as well." He looked away from his father's gaze. "Now we know how you feel about it, but Linda and I both think we may have a better chance of getting off the Island and across to England than you do!" There was a long pause as Jerry waited for his dad's reaction.

"And how, might I ask, have you managed to come to that conclusion?" asked Stan, focusing carefully on his son.

"Well," explained Jerry, "being children, for one thing, we won't be missed so much, especially with next week being the school holidays, and secondly, we have thought that the best place to leave is from the north coast by being lowered down the cliffs and as we are both smaller and lighter we reckon we could make it a lot easier than you."

"The cliffs!" his mother repeated in a panic as she walked into the kitchen from the hallway. "How on earth are you going to climb down those cliffs? Have you really thought about this sensibly?"

"Actually, yes," replied Jerry. "If you are there, we could be tied to the rope and abseil down. It will be much quicker and a lot safer than any other way."

"Um," mumbled Jerry's father. "How carefully have you thought about all this?"

"Oh, really carefully," replied Jerry calmly, "and we have prayed about it too."

"Well, let me ask you a few questions," said his father in a very serious voice. "Firstly, where do you propose to get a boat and an outboard motor, and secondly, where do you think you will be able to find a long enough rope to get you to the bottom of those cliffs?"

"Well, the rope we already have," Jerry replied eagerly.

"A rope?" quizzed his father. "You have a rope - where did that come from?"

"Well," answered Jerry, thinking hard how best to answer this difficult question. "Linda's father still has one stored in his barn but we measured it and it was too short so we, er, um, shall we say, borrowed one from the German Army."

"You borrowed one," his father exclaimed, in disbelief. "You borrowed a rope from the German Army! I don't believe it!"

"Well we did, although we have not yet measured it, but we think that if we tie both Linda's dad's rope and ours together we should have enough to allow us to reach the bottom of the cliffs."

Jerry's parents looked at each other in amazement. "Okay, you have a rope, but what about a boat? Don't tell me you have borrowed one of those from the German Navy!"

"No," answered Jerry in all seriousness. "I had rather hoped that we could have borrowed and used Uncle Fred's boat," he confessed.

"What, that old worm-eaten rowing boat? Why, that would never make it to Guernsey, never mind England, and anyway, I thought you were planning on leaving from the cliffs on the north, so how on earth will you get the boat to the bottom, lower it down on a rope first, I suppose?!" he said, with a degree of sarcasm in his voice.

"Yes sir," replied his son, with a note of triumph. "That is exactly how we intend to do it."

His father rolled his eyes upwards and continued, "So you're telling me that you intend to lower yourselves and Uncle Fred's boat down a sheer three hundred foot cliff and then motor all the way up the English Channel to England."

"Yes," replied Jerry simply. There was a long pause as again his parents looked across at each other.

"Well," his father said, after what seemed to Jerry an eternity, "we will have to discuss it with Linda's parents first and see how they feel. You see, son, I was warned yesterday that I was being watched closely by the Germans and told not to do anything silly. That rules me out from going, but just maybe you two young rascals with all your courage could just be able to give it a go." He stood up and ruffled his son's hair. "Well, we will have a chat with Susan and Nigel and see how they feel about letting Linda go, and we'll do it today as time is running out."

CHAPTER 9

Engines

"It's okay!" Linda shouted to Jerry across one of the hedges that bordered their farms as she ran across the field. "They have said I can go! Yippee!"

The two walked along either side of the hedge until they came to a gap where Jerry squeezed through to the other side.

"Your mum and dad came and spoke to my parents earlier and they all agreed that really, although they didn't want to, they were willing to let us both go as they thought there was no other alternative."

"Wow," gasped Jerry, "that praying really works!"

"Did you pray?" asked Linda.

"Yes, all night, and I was so surprised when Dad started to ask all these funny questions about what we had discussed and planned. I had no idea that he would not be able to go. Mind you, I do wonder why the Germans are watching him."

"Well, perhaps we need to be careful that they don't take too much interest in us either," suggested Linda. "That could well ruin the whole plan. Anyway what about heading off to see your Uncle Fred?"

"Good idea," said Jerry. "Let's go right now."

"Use my boat to go to England?" laughed Jerry's uncle. "My, this old thing could hardly make it to France and that's only twelve miles away. No, sorry, but it's too old and too weather-beaten to be of any good to you, and you say you need two engines? Well, you'll need a lot of good fortune to get one engine, never mind two, they're like gold dust."

On hearing this verdict, the two youngsters looked at the old man sadly. If Uncle Fred's boat was not seaworthy then where else could they get a boat? What would happen now to all their plans of escape to England with such important news?

Uncle Fred looked down at their sad and bewildered faces. Trying to lift their spirits, he said, "Mind you, Old Tom who lives down Gorey way near the green has a good engine, or at least I know he had one before the invasion, and I am sure he won't have given it up to the Germans, not Old Tom, he hates the Germans more than anyone on the Island. He will have to watch himself, will Old Tom, or he'll end up being deported before too long. Try him, but be careful; remember that 'walls have ears' and Tom is already in the bad books of some Germans for the things he's been saying about them, but if anyone can help you with engines, he can." He paused, and then added, "And I'll pray for guidance about a boat for you." The two thanked Jerry's uncle and immediately proceeded on the three-mile walk from St. Helier up the east coast towards Gorey.

They found Old Tom sitting in his garden eating a tomato he had just picked from the tomato plants that were growing in pots next to him.

"Hello," said Jerry. "My Uncle Fred has sent me to see you."

"Your Uncle Fred," came the response from the old gentleman. Linda looked at his bent frame and bronzed hands. She could see his face was furrowed and wrinkled underneath the old battered cloth cap he wore. "Aye lad, now which Uncle Fred would that be?"

"My Uncle Fred Le Marque," replied Jerry. "He's really my mother's uncle, not mine, but I've always known him as Uncle Fred."

"Oh, old Markey," responded the man. "He'll not have sent you to me less it were something important," he muttered. "What do ye want from me?"

Jerry and Linda looked around in case someone was

listening nearby; you never just knew who might be friends with the Germans. There were some, who having committed minor offences, had been put in prison because one or two of the Islanders, in exchange for money, cigarettes and various other luxuries, had informed on them to the Gestapo. In fact, Jerry was even wondering if he should have told his uncle their plan, as he felt that the least number of people who knew about it the better.

"Would you mind if we went inside, please?" asked Jerry.

"Just as you wish," the old man offered a smile as he rose from his work and made his way up to the front door.

"Maggie," he shouted into the house, "put the kettle on, we have two young visitors, and one is the nephew of Fred Le Marque."

The two children followed him inside and Jerry made sure he shut the door behind them. The old man signalled to them to sit down on a settee as his wife appeared from a door behind him.

"Hello," she said in a kindly manner, "so who is Fred's nephew?" Then as she realised there was only one boy present she corrected herself, "Oh, how silly of me, of course you must be," she said as she looked at Jerry. "So what's your name?"

Jerry spoke up, "Jerry Le Godel."

"Oh yes, you are Emily's son, from Carrefour Selous."

"Wow, how did you know that?" Jerry questioned.

"How old are you?! And yet you still don't realise that just about everyone knows everyone else here in Jersey," the old lady chuckled.

"Yes, I guess you're right," he replied. "We do all seem to know everybody and everyone's business."

"Well, what do you want to drink?" she enquired. "I don't have much really by way of children's stuff, just water or tea, unless you want milk. Thankfully we can still get plenty of milk, even with the Germans here!"

"Milk will do us fine," answered Linda.

Old Tom looked at the children a little impatiently. "Well,

now that business is out of the way, tell me what brings you here to me?"

"Outboard engines," said Linda, sliding to the edge of the settee on which she was sitting, and almost whispering her answer in a conspiratorial way. There were a few moments of silence as Tom took in her answer.

"Ah yes, outboard motors," he murmured. Then in a much more matter-of-fact way, he said, "And what about them?"

"We need one urgently," explained Jerry. "We need a motor, or even better, two motors and a boat, because we have to get to England!"

There was an awkward silence as Tom rubbed a finger round the collar of his shirt. "And just what makes you think that I have an outboard motor?" he asked.

"Uncle Fred told us," Jerry said with enthusiasm. "He said that you wouldn't have given it to the Germans because you hate them so much."

There was another awkward silence.

"So, just why do you want to get to England? Are you doing this for someone else?" the old man quizzed.

Linda spoke up, "If you don't mind we really don't want to say as we don't want too many people knowing, but if you do have an engine please tell us, and tell us if you will let us borrow it? If you say no to either of these questions we will just walk away and forget we were sent to you, but this is of such importance we don't want to waste any time."

Tom's wife appeared with the milk and a homemade biscuit each.

"Well," she interrupted, looking at her husband, "you always said that you'd only part with that engine if there was a real need. I don't know what it is, but knowing this 'ere boy's mother, I can guess that it must be important for him to come asking like this."

Silence filled the room as all eyes turned to Old Tom, waiting for a response from him.

Finally Old Tom spoke, "Aye, I have one, and a few spare

parts too, but I don't have a boat. I assume you will be using your uncle's."

"Unfortunately, Uncle Fred's boat is not seaworthy enough to get us to England," explained Jerry.

"Well, boats hereabouts are not easy to come by and so you may just have to take what comes. My engine will work so that's you halfway there, but you may have to manage with your uncle's boat." Again, there was another awkward silence.

"Well, when can we pick the engine up?" asked Linda eagerly.

"Aye, you'll just pick it up and walk home with it, will you?" Tom answered, with a wry grin. "No, I'll use my horse an' cart and bring it up myself, but not to your house, young man," he said, turning to Jerry. "I hear that the Germans are on the lookout for your father!"

CHAPTER 10

The Boat

Next day Linda awoke early. She knew that somehow, someway they had to get hold of a boat suitable for crossing to England safely. It had to be sturdy enough to negotiate some of the strong tides that prevailed around the Channel Islands and through the English Channel. As she lay in her bed thinking about all that had already taken place and all that still had to be done, she heard horse's hooves approaching and entering into the yard. She climbed out of bed and looked out of the bedroom window. She was surprised to see Old Tom atop of a small trap pulled by a chestnut-coloured horse. Dashing out of her bedroom and flying downstairs as fast as she could, she almost bumped into her father as she swung herself around the balustrade at the bottom of the stairs. Her father joined her at their front door and greeted the old man who was tying his horse loosely to a fence post.

"Well," said Tom, turning to Linda and her father and then cautiously looking around, "I've brought it along with a few spares I had knocking about. I'm told you're a right good mechanic, miss, so hopefully you can maintain this and it will do the job for you."

Linda's father looked between the two. "Sorry, I think I have missed something here," he said, with a frown upon his face. "Were you expecting something?" he asked, looking at his daughter.

"Oh yes," she said, as she gave a little cry of delight. "I'm sorry, Dad, but I forgot to tell you that we have been given an outboard motor to use when we leave the Island." The frown cleared from her father's face as he stepped forward to help

Tom lift some crates of tomatoes and bags of potatoes off the back of the trailer. Underneath was not just one engine, but two! One was much cleaner and newer than the other, and looked as if it had hardly been used.

"I had t'other one hidden away like," explained Old Tom, "and I guessed it might be useful when you said you wanted two."

"Oh yes!" Linda cried. "Two are much better than one in case one breaks down. I know a little about engines, but if we were stuck out there in the middle of the sea and it failed, I'd be scared that I would not have the right tools or spare parts."

"Well, now," interrupted her father, "stop the talking and let's get these into the barn where they can be hidden, at least for the time being." The two men lifted the motors off the back of the trailer and carried them into an adjacent barn. Linda followed with some of the 'spares' Tom had also brought.

"Will you stay for breakfast?" Linda asked.

"Thank you, but no, young lassie," Tom replied. "I'm on me way t'market and if I don't get there soon someone might ask some questions." He untied his horse from the fence and led it around to face the track away from the farm. Mounting the little trap he gave the reins a tug, and with a wave he was on his way. As he was turning past the farm, he looked back and called, "Good luck to you, young lass."

As Linda and her father walked back into the farmhouse, he said, "Well, I hope you two know what you are getting yourselves, and us, into. It's a dangerous thing you'll be doing and we will be heartbroken to see you go, especially not knowing what has become of you."

"It won't be easy for us either," she replied. "We don't want to go and leave you, but Hitler's visit will be such a big thing, especially if something could happen to him; it could save so many!"

"Yes, yes, I know, I know," answered her father, placing his hands on her shoulders and looking down at her with tears in his eyes. "If it wasn't that we know how vital this trip is, we would never have agreed to let you go." He pulled his daughter towards him and held her tight.

That afternoon Jerry and Linda headed to Uncle Fred's again to enquire about his boat.

"But I tell you it will sink before getting to England," Uncle Fred told them as they sought permission again to use his boat. "It's just too rickety and weather-beaten, this old thing." He looked lovingly at his fifteen-foot long boat. "I tell you, I know all the waters around this Island and they are some of the most dangerous in the world. This old boat here has sailed these waters, in the storms of winter, during the fearful spring tides and during the calm of summer, but she's not up to it anymore. Not now."

Jerry and Linda looked at each other despondently. "Surely we can fix it and make it watertight," Jerry suggested rather desperately.

"Ah, she's beyond that, my boy. Even if we did fix it, give it time and it'll sink just as sure as yon there Titanic did." His uncle put his hand up to his furrowed brow and gave it a scratch as he thought long and hard. "Mind you," he went on, "I think I might just have the answer to your problem. Old Mrs Renouf down in Georgetown, she has a boat that used to be her husband's, but he was killed down at the harbour when we were bombed just before the invasion. She might help. Leave it with me and I'll get back to you." With that, he put on his cap and headed in the direction of...well, the two could only guess, hopefully Mrs Renouf's house!

It was evening before Uncle Fred came cycling up to Jerry's father's house. He jumped off his rickety old bike and almost hopped through the front door. "I know that I shouldn't have come here," he said, "but I have a bit of news for you. I spoke to Mrs Renouf and you can have her boat, but it's a bit bigger than mine, it's twenty feet long!"

"Wowee!" said Jerry enthusiastically, jumping up and down with delight. "That'll be great."

There was a sudden silence, until his uncle continued,

"Longer length means a wider beam and both of those things mean more weight."

"Oh, I hadn't thought of that," said Jerry, suddenly calming down.

"And," went on his uncle, "it will be a lot harder to get it to where we want it. There are so many soldiers looking out for us. They will want to know what we are doing wheeling a twenty-foot boat around the Island."

"Yes, it's all going to look very suspicious, so it will, especially with me under surveillance by the Germans," added Jerry's father. They realised it was going to take some planning and a lot of care to get the boat they so desperately needed.

They went into the kitchen, and Jerry's mother put the kettle on the hotplate of the cooker and, opening its door, threw in some wood from a basket beside her.

"You know, Uncle Fred, we'd really rather these children didn't have to go. We have hardly slept for worrying about it. Even if they can get away from Jersey, it is still a hundred miles to safety and you know yourself just how unpredictable the English Channel can be." She struggled to contain her emotions.

Her husband came to her rescue. "What Emily is trying to ask, Uncle Fred, is would you be willing to go with the children to guide and help them? There are few men left in Jersey as knowledgeable as you about the tides around this Island, and I'm sure they'll need all the help they can get."

There was silence, which was broken only by the whistling of the kettle. "Aye, well, I have been thinking and praying about that myself," the older man replied earnestly. "Just this morning I was reading my Bible and I really felt the Lord speaking to me. I was thinking of these two youngsters and what they are hoping to accomplish, and as I read Isaiah chapter six the words 'Here am I, send me' seemed to stand out from the page. I will gladly go, and with God's help we will get the information through to England."

Jerry did not want to admit it, but he was mightily relieved to hear his uncle offer to come with them. Jerry had been thinking about the dangers of getting down the cliffs, and those of the sea. He was no sailor like his uncle and knew that he would have little idea which way to go. Having Uncle Fred on board would make all the difference.

Jerry could hardly wait for his walk down to school in the morning to tell Linda this turn of events.

"Wow! That's great." Linda jumped high into the air and punched it with both her fists.

"Looks like you have something great to tell the school," said the head teacher, Mrs Gresney, whom neither had noticed walking around the playground. "With a reaction like that it must be something good that Jerry has told you; something perhaps that you can share with the whole school. We could do with some good news for a change!"

"Oh," stammered Linda, unable to find a suitable answer, "it was nothing, nothing at all." Her words stuck in her throat as she tried desperately to think of an excuse to give her head teacher. "Er, um, ah, well," she finally said, "Jerry was just telling me that one of the sheep on his farm has had a lamb."

"A lamb!" exclaimed the startled teacher. "What, in July? That will be a first!" She dropped her glasses to the end of her nose and looked like an eagle about to pounce on its prey. "Well," she went on, "are you going to share this wonderful news with the school or just with me?"

"No, I don't think so. You see, it's just a private matter between the two of us," Jerry explained, trying very hard to redeem the situation.

"It seemed a bit more than that a minute ago when Linda was jumping up and down," commented Mrs Gresney. "Still, if you want it to remain between the two of you that's fine with me, but," she added seriously, "remember that 'walls have ears' so just be careful." With that, she walked away across the cobbled surface of the playground and into the school building.

"She's right," said Linda. "I should have been much

more careful and not have attracted so much attention to myself."

"I guess so," said Jerry, with a serious note in his voice. "We must take much more care how we act, and even what we say when we think we are by ourselves; you just never know who might be listening!"

CHAPTER 11

The Preparations

Following the incident at school, both youngsters took extra care when they were discussing their plans. They did not want to draw the unwelcome attention of the German authorities, the SS, or even worse, the Gestapo, to their plot. That could ruin everything and be the end of them and their families.

They had a meeting with both their parents at Linda's house in order to make some further arrangements. Uncle Fred, not wanting to attract any unnecessary attention to either him or the two families, didn't join them. He had, however, slipped a note into a paper bag filled with luscious home-grown strawberries which he had given to Jerry's mother earlier on in the town. In it he said that he was unable to think of a way to get the boat from St. Helier up to St. Lawrence without it looking suspicious, because transporting a twenty-foot boat over land would be a very hard thing indeed to explain to the Germans! He thought they should launch the boat off Green Island, the southeast tip of Jersey. How Uncle Fred intended getting the boat there he hadn't made clear, but the two families thought it could be an excellent idea. Linda and Jerry would then be able to meet him at their original launching point at the bottom of the cliffs at Devil's Hole, and by leaving from Green Island it also allowed the boat to be launched already filled with some of the supplies they would need for their journey. This, they could see, would be far easier than dropping all the things they needed down the cliff. Finally, he had added that he was busy working on a mast and sail which would be a help if they had any problems with the outboard motor. With his experience, he said that it shouldn't be a problem to take the little boat up the English Channel to the Isle of Wight or the south coast of England.

"Well," said Susan, Linda's mother, after reading the note aloud and throwing it into her wood burning stove, "your Uncle Fred hasn't left too much for you two to think about, has he?"

"Not with regards to the boat and its launching," commented Jerry's father, "but what about the engines that have been delivered here to your farm?" he said, turning to Linda's parents.

"You know, that's a very good point," Nigel, Linda's father, replied. "I don't think he's thought of that. We'll have to find a way of getting at least one of them to him and if we work it right, we should be able to lower the other engine down when we lower the children on the rope."

They were hoping Uncle Fred would launch the boat the following evening, or failing that, forty-eight hours from their meeting. The possible site for lowering the children down the cliff face was discussed in detail. All were in agreement that, despite the dangers, there was little option but to use the north coast as it would be the safest place for Uncle Fred to pick them up without the Germans seeing them. Stan suggested moving the pickup point further east than Devil's Hole to where the cliffs were slightly higher. From there, it would be much harder for anyone to spot the children being lowered down and it would be easier to watch for any Germans patrolling the area. Finally, it was decided that Linda's parents would check out the area the following day and report back.

The two families then made a list of other essentials that needed to be taken. The two mothers would do some baking and gather together as much as they could spare from their limited supplies. Fresh water needed to be bottled; a job for Jerry to do. A knife, matches and two lamps Stan would supply, and Emily would put together a first aid kit made up of some lengths of cloth roughly torn up into long strips and some liniment. It was agreed that the two ropes could be useful during the trip, and so once they were all safely in the boat they would then be dropped down to them.

Finally, it was suggested that Jerry and Linda should visit Uncle Fred as soon as they could in order to finalise all the arrangements.

They were all well aware that should anything go wrong at any stage, they would all be in very serious danger.

It was just before curfew time when Jerry and his parents left Linda's house and set off to walk the short distance to their home. Jerry was feeling a little subdued and his stomach knotted as he thought of what they were planning to do. For the first time the reality of the long distance from Jersey to England across the English Channel came into his mind. He wondered about how they would make it if the weather turned rough. What would happen if both engines broke down on them? What if they were spotted leaving the Island by the German patrols? If they were caught; what then? Would the tides take them too far out into the Atlantic Ocean? All these things and dozens more came flooding into his mind.

CHAPTER 12

The Arrest

Nigel and Susan decided to head out early next morning in order to investigate the best and safest place to get the two children down the cliffs.

"We must be careful," Nigel said to his wife as they walked along the narrow country lanes that led from their farmhouse north across the Island. "I don't think we will be able to avoid the patrols along the north coast, but as long as we don't look too interested in the area, they won't be suspicious."

"I suppose so," his wife acknowledged. "I just wish we had never embarked on this escapade, never mind allowing the children to get so involved. Oh Nigel, I am so scared!"

"Of course you are, my dear," her husband replied. "So am I. The children are really very brave; if they get away with this information they may well do a great deal to shorten the war and as a result save many hundreds, if not thousands, of lives."

The two walked on together until they reached St. John's Village and headed up towards Sorrel Point. They walked on past the Point, which was now out of bounds to anyone other than the German forces. They continued along a narrower road, which skirted the top of the cliffs, trying to keep as close as they dared to the cliffs without raising too much suspicion. Just as they were beginning to feel confident enough to turn off the road and head towards the cliff top, two German soldiers on bicycles came cycling towards them. They stopped and looked at the two as they walked.

One of the soldiers spoke. "Good morning," he said with a very heavy German accent. "Nice day today."

"Yes, very nice indeed," Nigel replied, trying to sound casual. "I think it may turn out to be a hot one."

"Yes, indeed," came the answer slowly, as if the soldier was searching for the right words with which to respond. "What are you doing?" he asked suspiciously.

"We are just out for a walk in the warm morning sun," Susan replied. "We always enjoyed our walks around the fields and lanes of Jersey before the war came and ruined so many things."

"Yes," replied the second soldier. "It is a pity that Germany was not allowed to take the land which is rightly ours." There was a hint of menace and disgust in his voice.

"You mean to say that Poland was rightly yours?" Nigel enquired boldly.

"Of course," the soldier answered. "Also Czechoslovakia and Hungary. They should all be under German control and our glorious Führer will make sure they are." Then looking at both of them carefully he demanded, "Your papers, please!"

As he waited for them to hand over their identity cards, he continued, "Your Prime Minister should have allowed our Führer more land and then all this would never have happened."

"If he had given you more land you would still have wanted more and more, no matter how much you were given," Susan replied with a touch of anger in her tone as she fumbled in her pocket for her identity papers.

"Ah well," came the reply again in faltering English, "we shall soon have..." He stopped again as he tried to find the right words. "...We shall soon take over the whole of Europe for the Führer."

Nigel and Susan handed over their identity cards to the nearest soldier.

"Um hum," he grunted as he read their names and details. "What are you doing up here?" he demanded.

"We are out walking," retorted Nigel, his voice now trembling with anger. "Can't you see that?"

"Ah yes," the German replied, with a hint of sarcasm. "We can see that, but why are you so far away from your home and what are you doing so near the cliffs?"

"We used to walk around this area before it was all controlled and restricted," Susan said with a sigh. "We love every part of our Island and don't take kindly to you coming and taking it over and telling us what we can and cannot do."

There was silence as the two soldiers handed their identity papers back and then hoisted their rifles onto their backs.

"Heil Hitler!" they said as they mounted their bicycles and peddled on down the road.

Susan and Nigel breathed a sigh of relief as the soldiers rode round the bend and out of sight.

"We must never forget," said Nigel confidently, "that British victory is certain!"

The two of them walked further along the road before jumping through a gap in the low hedge and across a small ditch onto the side of a field. They were now out of bounds. They kept crouched and as close as possible to the thick July foliage that bounded the field. Keeping their senses alert to possible danger they edged along the field and round the bottom towards the cliffs. As they neared the cliffs, they cautiously knelt to avoid being seen, and crawled on their hands and knees towards the gorse and bracken that marked the edge of the cliffs.

"Halt!" cried a loud voice from just behind them as they continued their slow crawl towards the cliff edge.

Susan and Nigel froze in blank horror as another command was given. "Stand up!" They both stood up very slowly; their hearts were beating fast and sweat appeared on their brows.

"Turn around!" another order was barked at them.

With a slow and careful movement, both turned to see their would-be interrogator. Two soldiers were pointing rifles in their direction, and a German Officer holding a revolver stood between them.

"Hands up!" the officer barked again. Both obediently

raised their hands. "That's better," he said in clear, crisp English. "Better to see who the lizards are that have been crawling around in the bracken!" His voice cracked with some amusement. "Search them." The soldiers immediately moved across and quickly frisked them,pulling out their identity papers, a few coins and a handkerchief as they did so. They walked back and handed the identity cards to the officer, who looked at the photos. "Um, you are quite a way from home, are you not, Mr and Mrs De La Haye?"

"Yes, we were out walking," said Nigel.

"A strange type of walking, I should think," the officer replied as he placed his revolver back in its holster. "I think you need to come along with us."

Nigel and Susan were marched across the field to the side of the road, where they were made to sit down with their hands on their heads. The German Officer spoke to one of the soldiers who then, shouldering his rifle, marched off down the road. The other soldier kept his rifle firmly pointed at them as they sat in dejected silence, wondering what would become of them, and the carefully made plans.

After what seemed like several hours, a grey lorry rattled its way up the road and drew up alongside where they were sitting. Two soldiers jumped out of the back and the German Officer ordered Nigel and Susan into the rear of the lorry. On climbing in they saw a couple more soldiers already seated in the back. These were the soldiers they had met on their bikes earlier on that morning! The two other soldiers jumped back in the lorry and closed up the small wooden drop-down door at the rear. The German Officer marched smartly around to the front and climbed into the cab next to the driver. With the door closed, the lorry crunched into gear, and moved off.

CHAPTER 13

What Now?

Linda had run round to Jerry's house so early the next morning that when she knocked on his door she found him still in his pyjamas. "Come on," she urged in her usual bubbly manner. "We have to get the supplies organised to take them down to Uncle Fred straight after school." Jerry looked at Linda as she stood in the doorway, her eyes sparkling and her face alight with excitement. "And it's the last day of school!"

"Well, you didn't need to get me up this early," he replied, glancing at the clock in the hallway which was showing ten past seven. He invited her in and mumbled in embarrassment, "I'd better get dressed."

"Morning, Linda!" a lively cry came from the kitchen. It was Jerry's mother, her arms covered up to her elbows in flour. "I am just baking some bits and pieces for you to take on your journey."

"Great," Linda replied as she walked into the kitchen and pulled out one of the chairs to sit at the old oak table. "Smells good to me," she said, taking a long sniff.

"And to me, too," Jerry shouted down from the top of the stairs.

"Mum and Dad have gone to take a look at the cliffs to try and find the best place for us to leave the Island," Linda said as she leaned back in the chair.

"I do hope they will be careful," replied Jerry's mother with a frown as she carried on kneading the bread dough on the table.

"Oh, I'm sure they will," answered Linda breezily as Jerry

appeared through the door, his hair standing up on one side of his head.

"You'll need to comb your hair before you go outside," his mother scolded.

Reluctantly, Jerry ran back upstairs to get a comb and ran it through his hair, not that it made an awful lot of difference!

"Okay," said Jerry's mother as she washed the flour off her arms under the taps of the kitchen sink. "I have almost everything ready that you will need."

She walked over to a large bread basket overflowing with various items which was sitting on one of the heavy wooden chairs. "Here," she said as she started to pass the contents to the two youngsters. "We have some linen cloth to make bandages, Dad's old penknife, and the last of our TCP disinfectant. Here are a couple of bottles, Jerry, that you can fill up with fresh water at Uncle Fred's; it would be a bit silly for you to carry the water halfway across the Island! There are a few tins of food, and some baking which should hopefully keep you going for a few days. Now, I suggest you parcel them up in those old potato bags."

Soon the two friends were sorted. They ate a quick breakfast and set off on their way to school.

Being the last day before the holidays, school finished slightly earlier. Normally Jerry and Linda would skip home gleefully. However, this afternoon they walked quickly but soberly as they discussed the final arrangements. They went to Jerry's house first to pick up the supplies in the potato bags, and then they walked along the winding lanes and green fields of the beautiful Jersey countryside. Although it was early afternoon, a light breeze kept the temperature low as they made their way thoughtfully across the Island. Neither of the two were strangers to walking. In fact, the majority of the Island's population did not even own a motor car at the beginning of the 1940s, and those who did had them taken by the German Army not long after they arrived. Many of these motor cars had been shipped to Europe to assist the Germans in their war effort there. Most of the Islanders could easily walk across the Island and back in a day. It was just something they did without giving it much thought. As the two walked on they continued to chat about the various plans and the dangers that faced them if things went wrong.

"I have heard that the Gestapo use pliers to pull your nails off," said Linda with a shudder.

"Well, from what I hear they do far worse than that," replied Jerry as they passed under some large trees leaning over the road.

"Umm.... Sure hope they don't catch us, I'm rather attached to my finger nails!" Linda said with a wry smile. Both children smiled, completely oblivious of the fact that Linda's parents had been picked up by the German Army.

Jerry and Linda arrived at the small cottage and walked up the short path to the front door, which was situated inside a brick archway. It had a bell pull cord, which did not work, so Jerry banged on the door. Within a couple of minutes, Uncle Fred appeared and peered through the glass in the door. Giving the rusty handle a mighty heave, he succeeded in opening it. "Bit stiff!" he said as he let the two inside. "I usually make use of the back door. Still, nice to see you. Come on in." The two walked in and plonked themselves down on the shabby settee with the bags of supplies beside them. Bits and pieces of wood lay on the table and some had fallen onto the floor. "Oh, I've been making a mast and a sail in case both outboard motors fail, then we can still get to England safely." Uncle Fred picked up some of the odds and ends from under the table, and sat on the nearest kitchen chair. "Well, have you come to discuss the final arrangements, and are those some of the supplies?" he eagerly enquired.

When Jerry nodded, he continued, "In fact, I thought we should go tomorrow night. There will be a full moon so we won't be fumbling around in the dark."

"We could always use torches," Jerry interjected with a cheeky grin.

"Well, if you want to get caught, then you're welcome to use one," Uncle Fred replied with a chuckle.

Jerry laughed back, "No chance of that!"

"We can't spend too much time larking around," Linda said, starting to laugh. "We must discuss the plans as we only have one more day until we set sail."

Uncle Fred told them that he would set off from Green Island at 11.45pm when the guard duty was being changed, and then he would sail around to the north cliffs to meet Jerry and Linda with the rest of the supplies.

"What do we do when we are all in the boat and out of danger from the Germans?" asked Jerry.

"We head north-north-east towards the Isle of Wight, which is just off the south coast of England." Uncle Fred proceeded to show them exactly where they were heading on a map he took down from the bookcase beside the fireplace.

"And from there to good old mainland England," Linda said, doing a mock salute, which made Jerry and Uncle Fred roar with laughter.

"Well, that's us organised then," Uncle Fred finally said when all the plans had been discussed, "but I think we should ask God for His help and guidance, as this is going to be a dangerous journey."

Jerry and Linda glanced at each other before closing their eyes and bowing their heads as Uncle Fred stood up to pray.

Once the prayer was finished Jerry asked, "How do you know that there really is a God?"

"Well now, that's a good question," his uncle replied. "If you had known me in my younger days you would have seen what a wild maniac I was; a sailor known as 'Fiery Fred' 'cause of my quick temper and liking for too much drink. One morning I was up on the mast of one of the ships, and due to the effects of the previous night's drinking I lost my balance and fell into the sea. I lost consciousness in the icy water and was just about to give up on life when one of the crew from the ship saw me and, with the help of the other sailors, managed to haul me back on board. That experience shocked me and after that I was determined to sort myself out, stop drinking and live a more respectable life. But when the temptation of a free drink came my way, there I was back in the taverns of the ports we entered and eventually having to be carried back to the ship by my mates. Years passed, and I still determined that one day I would get myself right but I never did.

"Then one day when we were in the port of Belfast during the last war, I remember hearing a man preaching in the street. I started laughing and jeering at him, but as I walked closer, I heard him tell of the love of God in sending His Son, the Lord Jesus, down from heaven in order to die for my sins. I was gripped by the fear of meeting this God I didn't know. That night I found myself on my bunk praying my heart out to God and pleading with Him to forgive my sin. The next day I went to find this man and see if he could help me sort my life out. He was not on the street where I had seen him the day before, but I saw a billboard advertising some meetings by a man called W P Nicholson which were starting that evening, so I went along. Well, I had never heard the like in my life. That man had us all laughing one minute and crying the next. I felt totally wretched as I thought of my drunken and wild life. Suddenly I realised, that despite my awful sin, God's Son had died to provide forgiveness and salvation for me. I wept as I heard for the first time of the sufferings of the Lord Jesus on the cross for me. There and then, sitting in yon church in Belfast, I trusted Christ as my Saviour."

"Wow," said Jerry, who together with Linda had been listening with rapt attention, "I never knew you were once a wild man, Uncle Fred."

"Aye, I once was, but I thank the Lord that now I am one of His precious lambs and He will never leave my side."

Jerry and Linda looked at Uncle Fred, waiting for him to explain what he meant, but instead he carried on.

"As I was sitting there in that church weeping, a man put his hand on my shoulder. I think he was amazed when I told him that I had trusted Jesus just a few minutes before. He and his wife took me back to their house and gave me supper. I had never before known such kindness. They even gave me a lovely black leather Bible. Then I heard the clock strike eleven and remembered my boat was about to set sail. I thanked the couple for their kindness and ran back through the city towards the docks. I arrived just as my ship was leaving the harbour and heading out into Belfast Lough. No doubt my chums had been looking for me in the inns and taverns of Belfast, expecting to find me drunk as usual. Having failed to find me they had set sail, leaving me behind."

"What did you do then?" asked Linda, looking up at him.

"I found my way back to the folks who had taken me back for supper and they kindly gave me a bed for the night. Next day I went down to the harbour to try to get a boat to Southampton so that I could get back on board my own ship. I worked my way back to the south of England as a stoker putting coals into the boilers of a steam ship. When we reached Southampton my boat was not there! I was told that it had encountered a German submarine, been torpedoed and sunk and that there were no survivors. So God not only saved my soul in Belfast, but my life as well!" Uncle Fred wiped a tear away as he finished his story.

"That's amazing!" Jerry finally gasped as the power of speech returned to him. He felt the hairs on the back of his neck stand on end. "Just amazing!"

About an hour had passed since they had first arrived at the cottage. Jerry and Linda were thinking it was time they returned home when there came a loud knock on the back door. All three jumped in fright, thinking it was the Germans. Uncle Fred peeped cautiously through the rear curtain as Jerry and Linda ducked behind the chairs. "It's only your mother, Jerry!" Uncle Fred sighed in relief.

Jerry got up and went to open the backdoor for her. His mother was hot and breathless as she ran in. She grabbed the chair that Linda was sitting on and exclaimed with a sob, "They've arrested your mum and dad!"

"What? My mum and dad, are you sure?" asked Linda in an unbelieving voice.

"Yes, the Germans came. I don't know what happened; I just

know that they were arrested. Stan's really worried because those engines are in your parents' outbuildings and if they find them your parents will have no chance of being released and you'll never get off the Island in the boat."

"Well, what are we going to do? We've got to get off the Island and get to England," exclaimed Jerry, a frown creasing his brow.

"Where have they taken them?" asked Linda calmly, trying to hide her emotions. She was trying very hard not to think about the conversation that she and Jerry had had earlier about fingernails and pliers.

"I really don't know, some sort of prison, I guess," replied Jerry's mum, reaching to give Linda a hug.

Uncle Fred looked glum as he tried to take control of the situation. "It looks very grim. We will have to think about what to do next..." His voice trailed off.

"I could try and make an engine," he suggested hopefully. "I have enough parts here and the knowledge to try it at least."

"But what about my mum and dad? What if the Germans find the engines and put Mum and Dad to death?" Linda said, breaking down in tears. Emily kept her arms around her, trying to bring some comfort to her.

"We have to get the engines before the Germans do," suggested Jerry, "but how do we do it without getting caught?"

CHAPTER 14

The Great Escape

"Old Tom!" Uncle Fred suddenly jumped up. "He has his horse and cart and we can hide the engine parts in the straw, so that the Germans will just think that we are delivering the straw to local farms."

"That's how he got the engines there in the first place," blubbered Linda through her tears.

"Then that's how we will have to get them back," said Uncle Fred. "We'll go and get him now, before the Germans search the house." Then he paused and added, "I think that it would be best if we put the matter to the Lord, because He will help us through in our time of need." They all bowed their heads again while Uncle Fred quickly prayed for Linda's parents and the safety of the engines.

When the prayer was over Jerry said, "Last time I prayed things worked out. It's sure to work again, so don't worry, Linda." Linda smiled gratefully through her tears. "Come on," he continued. "You and I will run up to Old Tom's and ask him to get up to your place with his horse and cart as quickly as he can. And..." he added with hope, "we'll keep praying as we go."

Without another word the two were out the back door and were running down the path, heading in the direction of Gorey, leaving Jerry's mother standing looking at Uncle Fred through watery eyes, drying her tearstained cheeks with the sleeve of her dress.

The two sprinted as fast as they could past the old Samarès manor house and along the inner coast road towards Gorey.

"Are you praying?" Jerry asked Linda, gasping for breath.

"Yes," Linda panted back, "I have been all the way!"

"Slow down a bit," cried Jerry after a while. "I've got the most awful stitch!"

"Try to ignore it so that we can get there as fast as we can." She ran on a few more yards and then, without looking back, shouted, "It's the only way to save Mum and Dad!"

Eventually they came to the coast road and were now walking more than running. They were almost at their destination! They crossed the road and ran across the green up to Old Tom's house. They hammered and banged on the door as if their lives depended on it. After what seemed an eternity, the door opened and Tom stood in the doorway.

"We need you to get the horse and cart as fast as you can and bring those motors back," Jerry blurted breathlessly in his haste.

"Mum and Dad have been arrested," Linda explained, "and we are sure that the Germans will raid our house. If they find those engines, Mum and Dad will be in big trouble! Oh, you must help! You must!"

Old Tom looked at the two thoughtfully and then said, "I'm not sure I understand, but you can tell me more on the way up to the farm in the 'orse and cart. I'll go and get the harness and then we'll be off." He ushered the two children in to the front room, and as Tom went out he said to his wife, "Trouble! Big trouble." She went to the kitchen, and reappeared a minute later with two tall glasses of ice-cold milk and some homemade cakes. The milk was great after their long, hard run and the two gulped it down in one go. The cakes followed in similar manner even though neither really felt much like eating.

"So, what's the trouble?" asked Tom's wife kindly, sitting down opposite the two.

"Linda's mum and dad have been arrested up on the north coast cliffs, and the two engines Tom left at their house are still there in one of the old buildings around the yard."

"Oh, I see," said the old lady.

"So we need to get them out as soon as possible, in case the place is searched," explained Linda.

"Well, I am sure Tom will do all he can to help you," said the old lady encouragingly.

After a few minutes, there was a commotion in the kitchen and Tom reappeared. "Right," he said, "let's be off."

They followed him out of the back door and along a lane, then up a rather steep path that eventually led out into another lane. They crossed over and found the horse quietly grazing in a small field. Further along a track that led to a farm Tom pointed out the two-wheeled trap. "You two fetch the trap and I'll harness the horse," he ordered. When Tom had hitched the horse to the trap, Tom and Linda climbed up onto the bench seat, while Jerry hopped into the back. Old Tom picked up a whip from the floor and cracked the air, and they started moving. He turned the horse out of the drive and onto a road. "We had better take the most direct route," he shouted above the 'clip-clop' of the horse's hooves. "The sooner we can get there the better."

Through the narrow twisting lanes of St. Martin to St. Martin's Church and then up towards Trinity they trotted. With time pressing, again Jerry wondered why, when they had walked this way so often, it had never before seemed as far as it did today. As they came round a sharp bend, they saw a troop of German soldiers just fifteen yards ahead of them. Tom pulled hard on the reins in order to quickly halt the horse; they desperately hoped that the speed in which they had trotted round the bend would not raise any suspicions with the German soldiers ahead of them. Thankfully the troop marched steadily on, unperturbed by their sudden appearance. The road was far too narrow for them to pass, so Tom reined the horse in and, trying to look as relaxed as possible, they walked along at a nice slow pace behind the troops.

After several minutes, the soldiers pulled into a small area where the road widened. This enabled them to gently trot past. Tom waited until the troops were well out of sight before he dared to quicken up the pace again. They then trotted out of Trinity and on into St. John without further incident.

As they turned left into the road that led to their respective farms all three gave a start as a German car pulled up behind them and then honked the horn. Tom pulled the rig into the gateway to a field and they watched as the car sped past.

A little farther down the road, Linda's house came into sight. As they neared the house all three felt their hearts stop as they saw the German car that had just passed them parked in Linda's courtyard alongside her dad's old tractor.

"Gosh," said Tom in a whisper, "we can't go in there, that's for sure."

"Oh yes, we can," answered Jerry confidently. "Well, at least Linda and I can.

"You drop us off and wait for us at La Rue de St. Laurent. Linda and I will try to get the engines and drag them across the fields to you without being seen. Hopefully those soldiers will search the house first before searching the outbuildings. If that's the case, we have a chance of getting those engines away before they start looking."

As there seemed to be no other option, the old man agreed, wishing them all the best as they hopped down from the cart. Tom reluctantly trotted on to the agreed waiting place.

Jerry and Linda made their way along the edge of the road and then across the farm entrance towards the field that led to the back of the barn where the two engines were stored. Linda suddenly whispered, "Jerry, I'm so very scared."

"So am I," he said, seeing Linda's tearstained face. "But did you see those words in a frame hanging in Uncle Fred's house?"

"No, I didn't."

"Well, it said, 'Fear thou not; for I am with thee', and I reckon it's from the Bible."

"So what?"

"Well, I'm not sure, but I think that maybe it means if we trust in God like my Uncle Fred we don't need to be afraid."

"Well, I'm still afraid."

"Yes, so am I. Come on." The two crept around to the rear door. Jerry tried the handle only to find it locked. "One of us will have to open it from the courtyard side," he whispered.

"Okay," answered Linda, "I'll have to go and do it."

"Why you?" asked Jerry, with a puzzled expression.

"Because it's my house and if I get caught, I have a reason to be here, but you don't." Jerry, realising that he could not argue with her, let her go.

Linda looked cautiously into the yard. No one was about. As quick as she could she ran, crouching low, around the front of the building and in through its open door. She dived down behind a wall panting heavily, more from fear than exertion. She breathed a sigh of relief when she saw the engines. Her thoughts momentarily went to her parents and questions flooded her mind. Where were they? What was happening to them? She suddenly remembered that poor Jerry was waiting at the rear door. She crawled over and reached up to the rusty bolt that secured it. It had been so long since the door had been used that the bolt had rusted almost solid. She pushed, pulled and attempted to wiggle it loose. Faintly she could hear Jerry trying to whisper from the other side.

"What's wrong? Hurry up," he hissed.

Linda lay on her back and tried to kick the bolt open. She missed and caught her ankle on the bolt. She grimaced as she looked at the graze on her leg. Desperately she looked around for some means to prise it loose but found nothing. Frantically, she lay on her back and kicked hard at the bolt again. This time she caught it well, and felt sure it had moved as dust flew off in response to her kick. She tried again, and again, kicking out as hard as she could at the small piece of metal that was stopping her from opening the door and getting the engines out. At last, with perspiration running down the sides of her face, she felt the lock give. What a relief!

Jerry pulled the door open and sunlight flooded in, throwing its golden rays on one of the two engines that stood propped up in the corner. Together they peered out of the building across the yard. With all the kicking Linda had done, they fully expected to see soldiers striding across towards them. Quickly Jerry got to work, lifting one of the engines. "Phew," he whispered, struggling to get it out the back door, "these are much heavier than I thought they'd be."

Linda grabbed the other engine and pulled it over the cobbled floor and out into the field, closing the door behind them. As quickly and quietly as they could, they dragged the engines across the dusty field and then pushed and pulled them through the hedge.

"Oh, I do hope that Tom has waited for us," Linda panted.

"He will have done," answered Jerry confidently, "unless, of course, he has had to move on because of the German soldiers."

Soon they caught sight of Old Tom who was sitting in the cart down the lane. They signalled to him and immediately he jumped down from the cart and helped them carry the engines the rest of the way, and lifted them into the back. Linda and Jerry hurled themselves into the cart and quickly covered the engines with the hay.

"Wow!" Jerry exclaimed, as the horse moved off. "That was scary."

"It certainly was," said Linda, looking behind her, fully expecting to see German soldiers running after them.

Tom turned the trap down various country lanes criss-crossing the Island before finally beginning the descent back into Gorey Village.

CHAPTER 15

With The Gestapo

Linda's parents had been taken in the back of the truck to the German Army headquarters at the Pomme d'Or Hotel where they were interrogated by a senior officer. They were struggling to explain to the officer why they had been crawling on their hands and knees so close to the cliffs. "This is not normal activity," he had declared, as he twiddled a letter opener in his hand.

"We were out walking," Nigel explained. "We have always loved that part of the Island. Before the Occupation we used to walk there all the time. We were on our hands and knees looking for flora and fauna. My wife has a flower press," he went on to clarify, "and so she collects wild flowers."

During the course of their interrogation, a tall menacing-looking man, who had no uniform but instead wore a long black coat, entered the room. He saluted the German soldier and greeted him with, "Heil Hitler."

"We wish to interview these two prisoners," he informed the officer.

The German soldier looked between Linda's parents and the man in the black leather trench coat as if he was unsure what to do.

"I have not yet finished my own questions," he replied in a frustrated voice.

"That is of no concern to me," the man said. "I have told you we want to interrogate these two, and we want them now!" His voice was threatening as he continued, "Please arrange to have them transported to Havre des Pas as soon as possible." With that, the man turned, snapped his heels together and marched out of the room.

"I am afraid," the German officer said, "that I have no choice but to hand you over to the Gestapo. I advise you to co-operate fully with them as their methods of er, um..." he struggled to find the right words, "...interrogation are not pleasant." He twiddled his letter opener even more, and added, "We believe that you were attempting to assist our enemy, therefore having received an order from a higher authority I have no option but to hand you over."

Nigel and Susan sat in silence as they were handcuffed and then led out of the building. They were pushed into the back of a small car with a soldier between them. The engine was started up, and they were driven off.

Once outside the Gestapo Headquarters in Havre des Pas they were dragged out of the car and marched along the short path to the front door of the large semi-detached building that before the war had been someone's home. They were pushed inside and met by two men in plain clothes.

The front door was banged shut and locked behind them. They now found themselves inside the house with an infamous reputation among the civilian population. They were struck by its silence as they were taken through the hallway towards the back of the house. One of the two men opened a door into a darkened room and said abruptly to Nigel, "Inside!" Nigel stepped inside, but had only gone about two paces when something hit him hard in the face.

Susan, who was still outside the room, shrieked, "Nigel!"

Nigel struggled to steady himself and stumbled backwards, falling up against the wall at the side of the door. Susan was then hauled into the room by the two men and made to sit on a plain wooden seat which had leather straps attached to the armrests. The darkness was intense and all she could make out were shadowy forms around her. She felt someone undo the handcuffs and secure her wrists in the leather straps on the chair arms. She could make out the sounds of her husband being picked up and shuffled across the floor to sit down somewhere in front of her. All was quiet for a few seconds. Then suddenly the darkness was pierced by a light shining directly into her face.

"Good afternoon, Mrs De La Haye," came a terrifying voice through the darkness. "We would like to know which resistance group you are working for and what you were doing crawling around on the north coast this morning?"

Susan, in a state of shock, sat for a moment in silence.

"What were you doing?" The pitch of his voice was raised, as the question was asked again.

"I...I," she stammered. "I, er...I mean, we were out walking."

"No," bellowed the interrogator from somewhere in the darkness. "You were out crawling, Mrs De La Haye, you were crawling! Why?"

"Well, it's hard to explain," she answered.

"Hard to explain! Why is it hard to explain? Were you searching for buried treasure?" the questioner asked, giving a short guffaw at the end of his sentence.

"No, we used to walk there and we wanted to see the cliffs again." Susan tried to sound calm, but inwardly she was terrified.

"You were getting ready to send signals to the enemy of the German people," the voice boomed again. "You wanted to send signals, didn't you, Mrs De La Haye?"

"No, no," she stammered. "That's not true at all."

"As my wife said, we were just out walking," Nigel's voice came from the dark shadows opposite her.

"Ah!" the menacing voice added. "You are now back with us, Mr De La Haye. Good, good! Now maybe you will tell us what you were up to this morning?"

"Walking," Nigel added simply, "and looking for wild flowers."

"Oh dear," came the voice again. "Why can you not make life simple for yourselves?" Then he called out, "Kurt!" The shadow of a person walked up to the chair in which Susan was bound. "I do not want Kurt to have to use these on your wife's nails," the man said to Nigel, holding a pair of pliers, "but I want some answers as to why you were crawling about on the cliffs, and I want them now!" Staring coldly at Susan, he said, "I will ask you one more time, which resistance group are you working for?"

Nigel saw his wife's terrified face as the man took hold of one of Susan's fingernails with the pliers.

"No!" Nigel shouted with all his might. "We have told you we were out walking and longed to see where we used to enjoy walking and sitting. That's all!"

At that moment the telephone in the adjacent room rang and the interrogator strode out. After a short conversation he returned, shining the torch once again into Susan's face. "Well, it seems that a search of your home has not revealed anything." There was a pause, and then he snarled, "Interrogation over," then another longer pause, "for now." With that, Susan's wrists were unstrapped from the chair and handcuffed behind her back.

To their great relief, Nigel and Susan were then escorted out of the dark room. They were taken downstairs into the hallway, and then on down another flight of stairs to what had once been a cellar. Here they were uncuffed and thrown together into a cell that the Germans had created below the level of the street. In one corner there was a single wooden chair and a bucket which was obviously the toilet. In another corner was a roughly-made wooden bed frame with no mattress, which was just big enough for one person to lie down and stretch out.

As the cell door clanged shut, they heard a voice saying, "Until the next time then." The key turned in the lock and the footsteps of their captors faded into the distance. All fell silent, except for the sound of their rapidly beating hearts.

"Oh darling," Susan sobbed, "what have we got ourselves into? What can we do now?"

CHAPTER 16

We Go Tomorrow

The next day Jerry roused himself from his bed and opened the curtains. The early morning sun flooded in through the window. He looked out across the countryside and then down at the shadows of the various farm buildings, created by the rising sun.

He thought of the wonderful life he had enjoyed in Jersey before the Germans had come. He thought back to the happy times he had spent with his friends playing on many of Jersey's golden beaches. He remembered the strange little English boy he had met on St. Brelade's beach who refused to get his toes wet. Would the English ever come back to enjoy their beaches? He thought of the times that he, along with a few school friends, had ventured out across the vast moonlike landscape of St. Clement's Bay in order to get to Seymour Tower. Then there was the crooked, toothless old lady out mussel picking, who had shown him and Linda the safest and shortest way out to the tower, avoiding the treacherous sinking sands in that area. He remembered how she had taught them to judge the incoming tide, which raced in with tremendous speed across the large expanse of that rocky southeast coast. He wondered what had happened to her. Did the Germans still allow her to collect the mussels on the beach? It had been her only livelihood.

He thought too of the fun and excitement he had had on the old Royal Jersey Golf Course, as he had searched for golf balls that had been lost by the golfers, and how he had been able on occasions to sell them back to them at the price of two for a penny.

He recalled the times he had cautiously worked his way through the reeds at St. Ouen's Pond, Jersey's largest expanse of fresh water, on the west of the Island, in the hope of seeing some young ducklings or some rare birds that had stopped to rest on their journeys either north or south.

All these wonderful memories flooded through his mind as he stood at his window looking out across the fields. Really, he thought, there is no nicer place to live than Jersey. He sighed, then stood straight. "We are going to get these things back!" he declared aloud. "Linda and I are going to England. We must and we will be liberated!"

Suddenly, he had to become a man, and help carry to England the most important message that he had ever had to carry. The entire course of the war possibly depended on the success of their mission.

"Jerry!" his father called.

"Oh, sorry," Jerry stammered in response as his father came into the room. "I was just thinking about...about all the fun things we used to do here before..." Again he stopped, this time wiping a tear away from his face, "...before the Germans came and ruined it all."

"I know," his father replied, with warmth in his voice, that Jerry knew only came when he was really concerned about something. "I feel so sorry for you being caught up in this mess and with so much resting on your getting safely to England. No one your age should have to bear such a burden." Jerry looked up into his father's weather-beaten face and saw that his eyes were glistening as he struggled to hold back the tears. "Oh, Jerry! Do be careful, and come back safely." Tears were now freely flowing down his cheeks. "You know you mean the world to your mother and me; having lost your brother we couldn't bear to lose you too."

"Brother!" Jerry exclaimed with a start. "Brother!" he repeated. "You mean...you mean...I had a brother?" Jerry promptly sat down on the end of his bed and stared at his father.

"Yes," his father said simply, "he would have been two years older than you."

"What happened to him?"

"He died," his father said softly. "He was just two days old." His voice trailed into a hoarse whisper. "We called him Roger but he...he never left the hospital."

Jerry looked into his father's sad face as he continued, "We knew there was something wrong as soon as he was born because the nurses took him away from your mother. We only saw him a couple of times after that." He turned and looked out of the window. "We had been so devastated at losing him that we kept it a secret from you, but last night your mum and I could hardly sleep at the thought of losing you too."

Jerry stood and gave his dad a firm hug. "Please don't worry, Dad, I'll be okay, I promise!" The two held each other tightly, both lost in their own thoughts as they looked out of Jerry's window as the sun continued to rise over the east of the Island.

"I thought you had come to get Jerry!" His mother's voice broke the silence, bringing father and son back to reality. "It's breakfast time," she scolded. "Or at least it was when you came to get Jerry," she added, with a hint of mischief in her voice.

"We're coming," said Jerry's father as he composed himself. "We have just been reminiscing about the past," he explained.

"Oh, you mean before the invasion," she said.

"Partly," replied Jerry, "but then Dad was asking me to keep myself safe, and he has told me...well, he has told me...about...about my brother." He rushed on, "He has told me about Roger." His mother's face went taut with pain. She turned quickly, and walked along the landing before proceeding down the stairs, saying bravely as she went, "Come on quickly and get your breakfasts!"

"I'm sorry, Dad," said Jerry. "Perhaps I should not have said anything."

"Well, even all these years later, it's still hard for your mother and I to talk about what happened," his father explained.

The two of them went down the stairs together and entered the kitchen just in time to see Jerry's mother dabbing at her eyes with her apron. They sat down as she produced some homemade bread along with some freshly made jam from the strawberries Uncle Fred grew in his garden.

"Oh, yummy!" exclaimed Jerry. "My favourite - fresh bread and fresh jam! Oh, Mum, you're the best!"

"I've made some for you to take with you to England," she said gladly, grateful that her son appreciated her simple home cooking. "Uncle Fred wants to meet you both at Mrs Renouf's lock-up garage in Georgetown," she went on without any emotion in her voice. "I think it's still on for tomorrow!"

"Tomorrow!" said Jerry, in a shocked voice. "I really didn't think we'd be going so soon!"

"You'll have to!" exclaimed his father. "From the rumours we hear, Hitler is due on the Island next week, and if it's left any longer you will never be able to get to England in time to warn them."

"Well, I guess it's now or never!" Jerry declared.

CHAPTER 17

Change Of Plan

Linda hardly slept that night in her grandparents' house. Knowing that her parents had already been arrested, she expected a pounding on the door at any moment and the Gestapo to come bursting into their quiet cottage to take her away as well. She wondered if the Germans were torturing her parents to try to make them betray the plans that she and Jerry had so carefully made.

Her mind was working overtime. All she could think was, *What if it doesn't work out? What if the Germans are waiting for us on the north coast cliffs as we are being lowered down? What if...* Her thoughts stopped dead. What if we are all killed?! What then? What if there really is a God, like Jerry's uncle is so sure about?

She was so pleased to see the sun rising up above the horizon at about five-thirty the next morning. At least with daylight some of the fear of being arrested faded. Still, she jumped at every unusual sound that came in through her slightly opened bedroom window. When she finally heard the heavy footfall of her grandfather a little later, she got up and dressed, glad the long night was finally over.

Breakfast seemed to take forever. "Best just to let the Germans have their way and keep your head down until the war is over," said her grandfather rather flatly, over a slice of toast.

"I don't rightly know why Susan and Nigel got caught up in anything," added Linda's grandmother. "It's all so pointless. I mean, what can we do here in Jersey surrounded by

Germans? Your grandfather is right; we just need to sit tight until the war is over."

Linda could hardly believe what she heard her elderly grandparents saying. "Sit tight!" she shouted, as she stood up and pushed her chair away from the table causing it to fall backwards against the stone wall. "Sit tight and do nothing, whilst German bombs fall on our friends, on our family and on our...." Words seemed to fail her as she tried to think of a suitable ending. "Allies," she added with a scowl, as she swept out of the kitchen leaving both her grandparents speechless. She stopped, turned back, and added with gusto, "Well, I intend to do something great to help defeat the Nazis and end this awful Occupation." With that, she turned and walked out into the fresh air of another glorious Jersey morning. The sun was rising high in the sky and she felt the heat from its rays upon her face and arms.

"Linda!" The sound of Jerry's voice came from down the lane. She saw Jerry nervously look about him as he approached the house, then lowering his voice, he said, "We go tonight."

Tonight, after all the plans, she thought, *tonight we will be going.*

"But," she said, tears welling up in her blue eyes, "what about Mum and Dad? Will I be able to see them before I go? Oh, Jerry! What if I never see them again?" She stood crying on Jerry's shoulder. Jerry awkwardly put his arm around her. He felt unsure how to really help her. This wasn't the strong, carefree Linda he was used to.

"That would almost be too much to bear," she continued to sob.

Jerry stammered as he tried to find the right words to comfort his friend. "I just hope that everything will work out," he added simply. "Come on, we need to find Uncle Fred."

Uncle Fred was in an old lock-up garage along a back street in Georgetown.

"Hello," Jerry said cheerily as they entered. "How are you today, Uncle?"

"Never mind me," the old man replied. "It's you I am sorry for, young lassie," he said, turning to Linda who was trying to be as brave as possible. "It's a rum thing to have had your parents captured. And up on the north coast there, too! We will have to change all our plans." His face drew into a frown and he pursed his lips whilst he thought. "We cannot risk anything up on that north coast, not now! Even if they haven't said anything, my guess is that the Germans will be posting extra patrols up there for the next few nights at least. Well, until Hitler has been and gone at any rate." His face shone, and Linda and Jerry detected a twinkle in his eye as he added, "We will just all have to leave from Green Island and hope for the best. It will save lowering you two down those cliffs with the rest of the stuff in any case." He stopped and gently rubbed his hand along the side of the boat that was lying in a cradle next to him. Then he added, "I want you two to bring as much of the stuff down here with you tonight as you can. Do you think you will be able to do that?"

"I guess so," answered Jerry, thinking about the weight of the rope that he and Linda had carried home from the German garage just a few nights before.

"Good," said his uncle. "But you two just be careful, because with Linda's parents already under arrest they might be on the lookout for Linda, especially if her parents have been forced to tell them anything."

"Okay," said Jerry. "We'll be very careful. We promise."

"Good lad," his uncle replied, smiling. "I have asked God to keep us all safe and help you two especially, and I am sure He will, for He promises in the Bible never to leave or forsake us."

"You really do believe every word in that book, don't you?" Linda commented.

"Yes, lass, I do. It's been my guide now for more years than I care to remember and God has never failed me. I still wake up every morning thinking that it's the most wonderful thing in the world to know the Lord Jesus as my Saviour and heaven as my home. Now away with you! You have lots to do and we'll have plenty of time to talk on our way up to England."

Jerry and Linda ran out of the garage door and bounded along St. Clement's Road as fast as their legs could carry them. It was not long, however, until they were out of breath.

"Let's not go the normal way," suggested Jerry. "If the Germans are following us, they'll not know all the back lanes of the Island like we do, and if we cut across country and go via Victoria Village we will definitely be able to shake off anyone following us in a car."

CHAPTER 18

Release

As they dropped down a back lane that led into Waterworks Valley, they saw a couple of German soldiers walking casually in the opposite direction. Jerry and Linda stopped, wondering what to do and how to avoid the two men. One of the soldiers turned and spotting the two children, he motioned to his friend.

"Good morning," one of them said, in his best broken English. "We are um, ahhh," he paused as he fumbled in his breast pocket for a little book, "...not on duty," he continued, after thumbing through a few pages.

The other added, "We are out walking, would you um, er... us join?"

Both Linda and Jerry were relieved to find that the two soldiers were at least friendly and although they needed all their time, they thought that to turn down such a request might arouse suspicion.

"Okay," Jerry said, "but not too far or our parents might worry about us."

"Ah, parents," said Karl, the younger of the two soldiers. "Yes, they worry, they write me and tell me they worry," he said, trying to pronounce his English words through his thick accent. "Both German and Jersey parents worry." There was silence as the four walked down the valley towards St. Aubin's Bay and in totally the opposite direction to which the two children wished to go.

"Do you live um, er...what is the word?" Again a pause as the soldier fumbled for the right word. "Ah! Near here?" he asked, as sudden inspiration came to him.

"Yes," replied Jerry cautiously. "Not far away." Then, sensing an opportunity to gain a little more information, Jerry asked, "Is it true that Adolf Hitler is going to come to Jersey soon?"

"Ah, yes," answered one of the soldiers. "Our grand Führer is due to arrive next week." He smiled down at the two youngsters. "He will arrive and say this is just one small step before planting his feet in England."

"Oh," answered Jerry, rather unenthusiastically. "And do you think that he will ever get to England?"

"Get to England, I not too sure," the soldier replied hesitantly. Then he stopped walking and added, "But the Führer has already decided to um, er...make an English palace his home when we finally invade England."

Linda joined in, "Which palace?"

"Oh, I not sure, but not Buckingham Palace," the soldier added. "I think it is one near Oxford."

"I don't know of any palaces near Oxford," answered Jerry truthfully.

"But anyway, we don't think you will ever invade England!" Linda added with a certain degree of gusto. The two Germans laughed and slapped each other on the back.

"There, Karl," said the older man to his friend. "They do not think so either." They both laughed again, and added, "Thank you for your time. Now you hurry home before parents worry!"

"Okay," answered Jerry, glad at last to have a reason to get on their way. "We will! Goodbye."

"Auf Wiedersehen," answered the two soldiers, as they walked off down the valley.

Jerry and Linda doubled back on themselves, then took a branch road that led up a rather steep lane towards St. Lawrence Church. "Wow," said Linda, "I was worried that they would keep us all day."

"Yes," Jerry answered, "so was I. Come on, let's get home and get started!"

They barged into the kitchen to be met by Jerry's mother,

her face beaming. "Great news," she said, with an excited air. "Your parents were released early this morning!"

"Whoopee!" screamed Linda, as she jumped for joy, nearly knocking over a vase that was standing next to her on a Welsh dresser. "I'll go up straight away to see them."

"Just be a bit careful," warned Jerry's father, as his large frame filled the kitchen door. "The Germans are no mugs and may well have released them either because they have talked, or in order to watch them and see who they have dealings with. That's why I have not been to see them and I don't think Jerry should either. They will be expecting you with your being their daughter. Find out all you can and then meet Jerry somewhere away from here to stop them becoming more interested in us than they should be. Off you go, do be careful, and give your parents our love."

"Okay," answered Linda cheerfully. "Jerry, I'll meet you by the school in two hours time." With that she skipped down the hallway and out into the yard, and ran homeward as fast as her thirteen-year-old legs would carry her. She ran across two fields, leapt over a ditch and vaulted the old wooden fence at the back of her house, before flying around the side of the barn and into the gravel courtyard where the old tractor sat. She sped across the courtyard, and flinging the front door open, entered like a whirlwind. Her mother had seen her coming and was waiting for her in the hallway.

"Oh Mother, Mother," Linda called, as she flew into her loving arms. "I was so worried about you! I thought I might never see you again."

"Hello, my dear," her father spoke as he descended the stairs. "We're alright. No need to worry over your mum and me."

"Oh, Dad," she said, the tears streaming down her face as she turned and threw her arms around him as he reached the bottom step. "Are you really both alright?" She held both parents tight in an iron grip, as if showing them that no matter what happened she would never let them go again.

"Honest, darling," her mother answered. "We are both fine."

"Come on," said her father at last. "Let's have a small snack of something, shall we?"

The next thirty minutes were taken up with question after question from Linda, along with answers and explanations from her parents. Despite being very scared, they had not been badly treated, except for her father's bruised cheek where he had been hit, and the threats of the sinister man in the interrogation room.

They told her they had been taken to the Gestapo house in Havre Des Pas, and yes, they had spent the night there in a cell, but no, they had not told the Gestapo anything about Linda and Jerry's plan to go to England. With each answer to her questions Linda breathed a big sigh of relief. Everything was still on, and the chance to change the outcome of the war still existed and rested with two children and an uncle living on a small forty-five square mile island called Jersey. "Do you think that you will be watched?" she finally asked her parents with an anxious tone in her voice.

"Most probably, yes," her father answered, "but what I cannot understand about all this is why the Germans did not find those two motor boat engines. They have completely ransacked the house and outbuildings, but never told us a thing about the engines. They must have been a dead giveaway that we were planning something."

"Well," Linda replied, "when we heard what had happened we came up here with Old Tom in his cart. When we arrived the Germans were busy in the house so Jerry and I crept round and opened the back door of the old barn and managed to get the motors out."

"You mean you took the motors through that old door?"

"Yes," said Linda with a smile.

"But that door has not been open in years," her father exclaimed.

"I know! I had to kick it open, at the same time praying that no one in the house would hear. Eventually it opened and we dragged the motors out and over the fields to where Old Tom was waiting for us on La Rue de St. Laurent."

Both Nigel and Susan looked at each other in silence, amazed at the sheer daring of their daughter.

"My word, darling," her mother's voice broke the stillness. "You and Jerry are wonderful; do you know what you two have done?"

Linda, unsure just how to answer, simply said, "No."

"You and Jerry have probably saved us from some really harsh treatment at the hands of the Gestapo." Her mother paused before letting out a big sigh. "What a terrible thing war is, it's at times like these that you need your family the most." Then pausing, she walked over to her daughter and hugging Linda, she added, "And I'll be losing my only daughter tonight."

CHAPTER 19

Plans

Linda met Jerry outside St. John's School as planned. "Do you think it's safe for me to go to your house?" she asked Jerry when she got there.

"Dad says that he thinks it should be, as long as you don't go straight there from your house," Jerry replied. "After all, we are friends and it would be strange if we did not visit each other's home. Come on, let's go! My parents are desperate for news about your mum and dad."

"They were just threatened a bit, my dad was thumped by something and they were both locked in a cell overnight, but apart from that they seem fine..." Linda explained to Stan and Emily.

"Oh, what a relief!" said Emily.

"I knew that they'd never say anything to the Germans," Stan said, as he sat at the big oak table reading a copy of the previous evening's Jersey Evening Post.

"They think that because we moved the engines, that saved them."

"Um, and I think they might be correct there," answered Jerry's father as he carefully folded his paper and placed it on the table. "They would have been wondering what two fully serviced and working motor boat engines were doing at Carrefour Selous so far from the sea."

"Oh, I have no doubt that we did the right thing, no matter how dangerous it was," Linda responded, with a confidence beyond her years. Then she added, "I'll have to pop back home again to collect some clothes and bits and pieces from Mum and Dad before we set off, so I'll tell them how relieved you are that they are back safe and well."

"Yes, please do that," Emily answered, a smile upon her lips.

Just then, there was a loud knocking at the front door and Stan went through the hallway to open it. He was followed back into the kitchen by a tall slim man in his mid-forties.

"This," Stan announced, "is Philip Bretton. He works with the Bailiff and has some important information for us."

"Well," said the newcomer, pulling up a seat, "I have heard that you are planning a little trip to England." Jerry and Linda were shocked to hear this. They had been so careful about who they told, and apart from their parents, Uncle Fred, and Old Tom and his wife, they had thought the plan was a secret. "Don't look so surprised that your father has confided in me, Jerry, because ever since the Germans arrived last year, the Bailiff has been seeking a way to get as much information as he can to England about the Occupation and the German garrisons on the Island, so we are hoping you may be able to help us."

Jerry looked between his parents, Linda and Mr Bretton. "We will if we can," he answered, still surprised that someone else knew about their plans.

"Good," answered Mr Bretton. "We have drawn up some plans that we wish you to take with you." He pulled some pieces of folded paper from an inside pocket of his jacket and placed them on the table. "These pieces of paper show which beaches have been mined, as well as the machine gun posts at the airport and where we believe the Germans intend to construct gun emplacements around the Island." Opening out another small sheet, he then added, "This shows our estimates as to the number of troops on the Island as well as who is stationed where, and in which hotels, and information like that." He produced yet another piece of paper and carefully unfolded it, pressing the creases flat as he did so. "This one," he added, "is a rough map of St. Helier showing which properties and hotels are being used by the Germans." He looked around as a frown fell across his face. "If," he added, "you are in danger of being caught by the Germans it would be in your own interests to get rid of or destroy these as quickly as possible. If the Germans find these on you, you will be in BIG trouble," he warned.

"Okay," Jerry gulped. "I just hope we don't have to swallow all this stuff, like they do in books." They all laughed at Jerry's comment.

"Good lad," said Mr Bretton. "The Bailiff has asked me to send you his good wishes on your trip. May God be with you!" With that, Mr Bretton stood up, shook hands with each of them and turned and walked down the hallway and out of the front door. Jerry's father went and waved him off before closing the front door and returning to the kitchen.

"Well," laughed Jerry to his father, "you never were very good at keeping secrets, were you?"

Jerry and his mum and dad got together the final few items along with some extra clothes and warm blankets. Linda skipped out of the house as if she didn't have a care in the world as she headed back to her parents' house to gather up her own provisions for the long and hazardous voyage. No one could see it, but Linda's heart was as heavy as a sack of Jersey Royal potatoes as she made her way to say goodbye to her parents. *Whatever does the future have in store?* she wondered.

An hour later Linda was back at Jerry's house and almost everything was prepared and ready. The children knew it was time to commence their last journey down into St. Helier for some time.

Jerry desperately wanted to be brave but the closer the time came, the harder he found it to hold back the tears.

Linda noticed and tried to console him. "Go ahead and cry," she encouraged him. "I have just spent half an hour with my mum and dad just sobbing my heart out and they were doing the same. There's no point holding it in, it's tonight we have to be strong," she went on, "when we finally leave the Island

and are on our own with your uncle. Now is the time to let your emotions out, not then."

Jerry put the small package of clothes he was carrying on the oak sideboard as his mother came in and threw her arms around both children. The three stood in a long embrace, tears flowing freely, until Jerry's father disturbed the scene by saying, "Well, are you going to get on with the job or shall we stand here all day crying our eyes out?"

Jerry, taken aback by his father's curt manner, turned to look at him. He saw his father's own tearstained cheeks and realised that he too was overcome by the frightening reality that their plans were now beginning to happen.

Eventually everything was packed into Jerry's old pram, including the rope. The two were ready to meet up with Uncle Fred down in St. Helier. It was not at all as easy as Jerry thought it would be to say goodbye, and his legs felt like jelly as he and Linda walked off down the drive and away from the house that had been his home for the past fourteen years.

CHAPTER 20

Setting Off

Both children were pleased to be out on the narrow lanes of Jersey knowing that they had just overcome one of the biggest hurdles of the whole adventure – that of saying goodbye to their respective parents. Now as they set off on their great adventure, they knew that another big hurdle lay before them: getting past the German guards and out to sea in their boat along with Uncle Fred, and then the long and treacherous voyage across the English Channel. The day had become overcast but it was still warm. There was a slight breeze blowing across the sea from France which could make launching the boat from the south-east side of the Island all the harder. Jerry knew that breezes meant sea swells and he wondered how the three of them would cope if the boat was constantly pitching up and down. They made their way to St. Helier by the usual route of zigzagging across the beautiful Jersey countryside along the numerous narrow lanes that dissected the Island. As they continued their journey to the top of Queen's Road, they caught sight of St. Helier below. Here they stopped to look out over the town towards the lovely, but imposing, Elizabeth Castle, that stood as a sentry into the little harbour of St. Helier.

"Isn't it beautiful?" Linda whispered to Jerry.

"Yes," he agreed. "I cannot think of anywhere I would rather live than Jersey." He paused and then kicked out viciously at a stone on the ground, sending it flying through the air. "Except that it's all been ruined by Adolf Hitler and his rotten troops," he added, spitting out the name 'Adolf Hitler' in disgust.

They both stood in silence before Linda said, "Come on, we need to keep going."

They arrived at the lock-up garage where Mrs Renouf's boat was and pushed the pram up to the garage. A door opened and Uncle Fred appeared, frowning. "Come in," he said urgently. "Come in." The two stepped inside and walked up to the side of the little boat.

"We have a small problem," Uncle Fred explained. "I had been storing up some cans of diesel that I," he paused, as if looking for the correct word, "shall we say, obtained from one source or another, but last night the shed in which I was keeping it was broken into and most of the cans were taken, so we don't have enough diesel to get us to England." Linda and Jerry looked at each other and then at Jerry's uncle as the horror of the situation began to dawn on them.

"Who did it?" asked Jerry with a trembling voice.

"I really have no idea," his uncle replied as he walked around to the far side of the boat. "All I know is that the lock was forced open and the cans of diesel were taken. Thankfully they left two, which will at least give us a start, but not much more."

Jerry let out a long sigh, "Well, what can we do?"

His uncle had by now climbed into the boat and was lifting up a large pole with a cross piece of wood attached to it.

"Well, I have fixed up this mast which will take a sail," he said, his face brightening. "I had already made it as I know how temperamental these engines can be. However, I have another idea." He paused as he placed the mast back into the bottom of the boat and stood up. "We will make a detour across to Guernsey and try to pick up some diesel there. I know that Guernsey is occupied as well, but if we can land at the right place and climb up the south coast cliffs, I have a very good friend who farms that area and I know he will be willing to help us."

Linda screwed her face up, "But won't the Germans have guards set up along the cliff top just like they do on our north coast cliffs here in Jersey?"

"Possibly they do, but if we are to get to England that is just a risk we will have to take," Jerry's uncle replied. "Anyway, let's get everything loaded on board and then get ready to move the boat out as soon as darkness falls."

They spent the afternoon packing the boat. There was the rope that Linda and Jerry had so bravely taken from the German lock-up. There were also the various bits and pieces of food that their parents had provided for them. There was a flash lamp, extra clothes, a couple of blankets and pillows, some tools in a small wooden box, the extra engine, the two cans of diesel that they had left, the sail, many bottles of water and a box that Uncle Fred had packed himself with what he termed 'essential items' in it. Things like matches, a candle, pieces of string and various other seemingly odd bits and pieces, and right in the middle a small, old, worn Bible. With the boat packed and the top covered, the three of them walked to Uncle Fred's house. Once inside, Uncle Fred made potatoes, spam and carrots for tea. After he had prayed, giving thanks to God for the food, the three tucked in with relish as Linda posed the question, "I wonder how long it will be until we are able to eat like this again?"

No one answered, as they all knew that it could be several days before they made it all the way to England. First, though, they had to get off the Island!

CHAPTER 21

To The Sea

The sun was just starting to drop below the horizon when Uncle Fred thought it safe enough to make a move with the boat. Old Tom had arrived about half an hour before to give a hand manoeuvring the larger-than-expected boat through to the launching point off the coast at Green Island. Uncle Fred had placed a map of the town and outlying areas on the table, and carefully talked through every street and lane, and every twist and turn that they would take to the launching site. Uncle Fred had been more than thorough in his planning and arranging of this trip. He had marked out where every German patrol would be and at what time, and the danger areas for meeting lone German soldiers out walking whilst off duty. He had even marked the houses where he thought neighbours might be unhelpful to them if they saw them moving the boat.

"Remember," he said to all very solemnly, "the boat is not ours and we are just taking it from Mrs Renouf to her friends in Grouville, if anyone asks any questions. We must be very careful at every place so as to at least get to Green Island without any hiccups."

Then lifting up a Bible, he flicked through the pages. "I found these verses in my daily Bible reading this morning." He looked at them over the top of the open Bible. "They are found in the prophet Isaiah. 'Fear not: for I have redeemed thee, I have called thee by thy name; thou art mine. When thou passest through the waters, I will be with thee; and through the rivers, they shall not overflow thee: when thou walkest through the fire, thou shalt not be burned; neither shall the flame kindle upon thee. For I am the Lord thy God, the Holy One of Israel, thy Saviour.' " He looked up from the Bible and said, "I believe that this is a promise from God that He will grant us His safety as we pass through the waters."

"That really is just amazing," Jerry said, almost under his breath, "to think there is a part of the Bible that talks about passing through waters!"

"There are so many things in the Bible that we should take great notice of," his uncle said. "I believe that this really is God's Word and that we need to obey it to be wise, practise it to be right and believe it to be saved."

"I never thought of the Bible in that way," Linda confided. "I mean, in a way that God can speak to me from. I just thought it was a dry, old history book."

"Nay, lass," Uncle Fred said. "It's anything but dry. Above all, it tells us the way to heaven through trusting the Lord Jesus, which is so important." He looked tenderly at them and then said with determination, "Come on, let's get going!"

Carefully they set off from Uncle Fred's house in two groups of two so as to avoid any suspicions as they walked the half-mile back to Mrs Renouf's garage.

Once there, Uncle Fred lifted up the iron floor bolts on the garage doors and swung the big wooden cross batten up. He then pushed one door a little and cautiously looked outside. All was clear, so he shoved both doors open and they pushed the boat on its little wheeled cradle out of the garage and onto the lane behind the house. One of the wheels started to make a squeaking noise as soon as it was out of the garage. Uncle Fred quickly stopped the boat and whispered, "That's no good." He went back into the garage and reappeared with a can of grease. He climbed under the boat and started to rub the grease into the wheel bearings of the trolley. That done, he placed the grease can back in the garage and pulled an old rag from off the shelf in order to clean his hands.

"Should have thought of that before now," he grumbled to himself as he vigorously rubbed the remnants of the grease off his hands. Uncle Fred carefully closed the garage doors behind him, bolting them from the inside and returning out through the back door and up the little path.

The boat was larger than the children had realised and it was hard to keep it in a straight line; the little trolley underneath seemed to have a mind of its own and kept veering off in different directions. Uncle Fred took up his position at the front and Old Tom pushed and steered at the back, with Linda and Jerry pushing at either side of the wooden boat.

When they came to the end of the little lane, Uncle Fred signalled to stop pushing. He looked carefully up and down the main road that they had to cross in order to continue their journey to the sea. Once he was sure that all was clear, he gave a wave. They strained, pushing the boat as quickly as they could across to the other side of the road, then continued along another back lane behind a row of terraced houses with long back gardens.

As they carried on manoeuvring the boat up the lane in the rapidly advancing darkness, a voice suddenly penetrated the air. "Nice night for a boat trip!"

All four stopped dead as an old man shuffled up the path of his garden towards the little group.

"Whatever you're up to, I wish you every success," he said as he came closer. As he reached the end of his garden path, the four saw his old wizened and wrinkled face smiling at them. "I just wish I was coming with you," he added, "as I doubt I'll be around to see the end of the Occupation, and our Island free again." His kindly old face looked forlornly at the little group as he gazed longingly at the boat. "Now, hurry along," he scolded. "You don't want the Jerries to catch you chit-chatting with me!"

They kept on pushing the boat in silence, leaving the old man leaning on his gate.

"Do you think he might tell on us?" whispered Linda to Uncle Fred through the darkness.

"Who, Stan Cormeron?" enquired Uncle Fred. "Not a chance! He fought the Germans in the last war and hates them more than anything. Guess he'd love to be coming with us. It just goes to show, though, how easy we are to spot and how conspicuous we are. We must keep our eyes and ears open."

The little party made their way perilously through the back roads and lanes of Georgetown, and then across a lane through a field towards the Manor House at Samarès.

Then came the most difficult and dangerous part. They now had about a quarter of a mile to negotiate along the main inner coast road at St. Clements, before reaching another small side road which lead down to the other main road that ran along the coastline. As they proceeded very cautiously along the inner coast road, Jerry suddenly called out, "I hear something coming." They all stopped to listen as in the distance the faint drone of an approaching motorcycle could be heard.

"Quick," said Old Tom. "Up to that gate on the left. Try and push the boat into the field." As they rolled the boat towards the gate Linda was gripped with a real sense of panic for the first time. While the distant roar of the motorcycle increased with every second that passed, Uncle Fred grabbed the handle of the gate and pulled it sharply towards him, praying that it was not locked. With a sigh of relief, he swung the gate open. There was no time to hide the boat behind the wall or shut the gate, as the motorcycle came into view and sped towards where they had just been walking. The four of them just managed to fling themselves to the ground behind the wall as the motorbike, ridden by a German soldier, flashed past in the darkness. The rider did not notice the open gate or the stern of the boat filling the opening into the field as he raced past in the direction of the town. All four lay in the field for some time, panting from both exertion and fear at the close shave they had just had. After several minutes, they carefully got up and crept to the road to check all was clear again.

As they started to push the boat out of the field they realised, to their dismay, that its wheels were bogged down in the wet, sticky soil of the recently ploughed field. Amid much grunting and groaning in their efforts, the boat eventually became unstuck, and they dragged it back onto the road, leaving muddy tracks behind. They were glad when Uncle Fred signalled for them to turn off the road and down the narrow back lane that would lead them almost to their launching place at Green Island.

"I wonder what our parents are thinking right now," asked Linda in hushed tones.

"If they feel anything like me," responded Jerry, "they will be worried sick!"

"I guess you're right," Linda replied, "and at least we know what's going on, whereas they have no idea."

"Hush now," warned Jerry's uncle. "We are nearly there." He waved his hand in a silencing motion and then leaned back against the bow of the boat in order to bring its slow crawl to a halt. "Right, wait here whilst I go and check on the sentries down there. You remain quiet and keep a look out." Uncle Fred stooped down, and with a surprising amount of agility for an old man, he dodged around a wall and ran across the main coast road, before jumping over a low wall and into the garden of a small cottage close to the little lane that led to their planned launching point. As Jerry saw his uncle disappear, he remembered the heady days before the occupation when he and some of his school friends had picnicked on the small hillock called Green Island. They had watched the tide racing in across the lunar landscape that made up the beach at that part of the Island. There had been no need for the checking of areas in those days. All was open and accessible for adventurous children who loved the beach and rock pools. How Jerry wished once again that the Island could return to normality.

CHAPTER 22

The Adventure Begins

After about five minutes, Uncle Fred's tall, lean form came into view once again around the corner of the house. At first it gave the three a scare until they recognised his silhouette in the darkness.

"Okay," he said, "it's guard changing time and it seems that things are on our side as they seem to be changing guard right up at the far end of their patrol, so it's now or never!" Then, taking hold once again of the bow of the boat, he said, "Come on, let's go." They began to pull and push with all their might again. As they entered the short and narrow lane that led to the beach at Green Island, Uncle Fred signalled to them to stop again. He walked back to Old Tom at the rear of the boat. "No point in you risking things any further," he said. "You head back now and take care."

The old man looked up sadly into Fred's face. "No, I want to see you off," he answered determinedly.

"But it's too dangerous," argued Fred.

"Once you are in the sea, I'll go," Old Tom said defiantly, leaving no room for further argument.

With that, Uncle Fred walked down from the boat and cautiously checked both sides of the path. He ran back and said, "Okay, let's uncover the boat." All four unclipped the canvas cover. Fred and Tom folded it up with a speed and skill that impressed the two youngsters, and threw it into the bottom of the boat.

"Right," instructed Uncle Fred, "push as hard as you can, and don't stop until the boat is in the sea. All together now! Push!" The boat ran fast down the slight incline of the road towards the beach, gathering speed as it went. Linda and Jerry, each still on either side of the boat, fought hard to keep the boat heading in the right direction. They managed to turn it just before it ran onto the wet sand of the now receding tide. The boat slowed as the sand stuck to the wheels, but it kept going until finally they reached the water's edge. With a splash, the trolley rolled into the water and slowed to a stop. Uncle Fred, Linda, Jerry and Old Tom pushed the boat for all it was worth until it floated free of the little wheeled trolley, which was now totally submerged in the water. They pushed the boat out into the cold and dark expanse of ocean, until the water reached up to Linda's and Jerry's tummies. Uncle Fred whispered loudly, "Quick! Climb in!" Both of them hauled themselves up and over the side, and into the boat. Uncle Fred moved from the bow to the side and pulled himself in as well. He found the oars that were stored in the bottom of the boat, placed them skilfully over the side and slid them silently into the water.

Old Tom whispered, "Good Luck," as Uncle Fred began to row the boat away from the Island and out to sea.

Uncle Fred, in a hoarse whisper, replied, "Thank you for everything and take care, Tom."

The rapidly retreating tide gave the boat a little extra momentum as Uncle Fred pulled effortlessly at the oars and they began their journey out into the open sea.

The three of them watched Old Tom walk carefully out of the water and cautiously make his way up the beach until he disappeared into the darkness. As the boat made steady progress out and away from the shore Linda and Jerry suddenly felt very much alone.

"We must be careful around here," Jerry's uncle whispered. "This is a very rocky area and with the tide going out many of the rocks will be just beneath the surface. We are bound to scrape a few whilst rowing, but hopefully not too many if I can keep a sensible course. You two keep your eyes and ears open for any activity, either on the shore or on the sea."

The stillness of the night was broken only by the gentle

sounds of the waves lapping upon the distant shore, and the gentle but rhythmic 'splish splash' of the oars as they passed quietly in and out of the water.

With the cold expanse of ocean all around them and the night now so still, it was hard for the two children to appreciate fully that they had at last embarked on a real live adventure. Everything seemed so unreal and they both felt that any moment they would wake up to find it was only some great dream.

CHAPTER 23

All At Sea

Uncle Fred worked hard at the oars of the boat and slowly, very slowly, it made its way farther away from the shore and the dangerous rocks that guarded the south-east corner of the Island. Out of the dark gloom, the children could see the unmistakable outline of Seymour Tower rise out of the sea as they approached its eerie form. Before the occupation Jerry had played many times in the old stone tower during low tide. Now he thought about how lonely and bleak the tower looked. He knew that most of the beaches were now no-go areas in Jersey. One day, possibly quite soon, that would change!

As they rounded the southernmost tip of St. Clements, Uncle Fred spoke, "Right, it's time to start the engine." He placed the oars in their sockets and carefully made his way to the engine that was at the rear of the boat. He fiddled about with several knobs and levers before priming it with fuel. As he did so, he froze as he heard a noise in the distance that could only be a motor. The children heard it too, and with sudden terror threw themselves onto the wooden floor of the boat.

"Stay there and don't make a sound," said Jerry's uncle as he slid down beside them. The noise grew rapidly louder as the boat approached from the direction of France.

"I reckon," whispered Fred, "that it's a small supply boat coming over from Granville with some basic provisions." He paused and then added, "At least, let's hope and pray that it is, and not a patrol boat." With hearts beating hard they lay in the bottom of the boat. The drone of the engine grew louder and louder. Fred cautiously looked out over the side of the boat and saw the small coaster pass by about two hundred feet away from them. "Phew," he breathed, as the boat disappeared into the distance. "I was right; it's just a supply boat heading into St. Helier!"

Uncle Fred once more took up his position at the stern of the boat as he again prepared to start the outboard motor. Both Jerry and Linda knew that these types of engines could be notoriously difficult to operate even in the best of conditions and were delighted when it finally started. With the engine now working, the boat began to pick up speed and move much more rapidly through the water. Both Jerry and Linda felt a surge of delight as they felt the coolness of the night breeze on their excited faces. They carefully surveyed the outline of their beloved Island as the boat made its way up Jersey's east coast. The black mass of Mont Orgueil Castle could be faintly seen in the distance, the dungeons of which were the 'final home' of many who, in the past, had sought to capture the Island. Once beyond the castle, they would be out of sight of land.

As they headed for the north-east corner around Rozel, a sudden shaft of light flashed across the open sea in front of them. Uncle Fred had steered too close to the Island and the sound of the motor had been heard by the guards manning the searchlight at St. Catherine's. Uncle Fred steered the boat out again away from the land, as the beam of light danced across the wide expanse of water. Suddenly, the searchlight picked out the boat as it passed on a sweep, and after passing stopped and came back towards them. "Everyone down," Fred called, with urgency and alarm. Once more they dived to the floor, just as the bright beam from the searchlight picked out the boat a second time. Fred kept his hand on the tiller, still steering further away from the Island. He decided to take the risk of opening up the throttle to full, so the boat picked up more speed and cleared them of the searchlight. Just as he did, they heard an unmistakable clatter as a machine gun from the shore opened up, and they quickly ducked as the bullets splashed behind the boat. Through the noise, they heard Fred say, "We are out of range of those guns, but they may well try to blast us out of the water, so hold on."

He began to steer a zigzag course through the sea. The boat bobbed and weaved across the top of the prevailing swell. The German soldiers manning the searchlight failed to keep the rapidly disappearing boat in their view, as it manoeuvred first right and then left out of the range of the light. Suddenly there was a bang from the direction of the shore and the three looked up to see a trail of light launch up into the night sky, followed by a blinding flash as a star shell burst high above them, its light illuminating the area all around as it slowly floated down onto the water. This was immediately followed by a loud 'boom, boom, boom' from the shore, as a couple of heavier guns opened fire. "Let's hope they don't get our range," called Uncle Fred as he masterfully manoeuvred the little boat through the dark, forbidding sea. Suddenly a shell splashed about a hundred yards off to the left. Then another followed it. Uncle Fred swung the tiller and steered the boat further away from the splashes. All the time the little engine kept up its droning, taking the three farther away from their Island.

After what was perhaps only a couple of minutes, the boat was out of reach of the searchlight, and the pounding of the artillery from the shore ceased, having now no recognisable target to aim at.

"What are we going to do now?" asked Linda, trying to put on a brave face despite being terrified.

"Well, first of all, we need to throw overboard some of the things we can do without," Fred replied in a solemn tone. "Then if they find these bits they might just think they hit us with one of their shells. Then we're heading straight for Guernsey! The course we are currently on will make the Germans think that we are heading straight for England, so if we turn north by west and make for Guernsey as planned we might just outfox them when their patrol boat comes searching for us." He paused as he adjusted the fuel valve on the engine. "Let's hope so anyway!"

With that, the three began sorting bits and pieces from the boat. They filled the engine with fuel in order to empty one of the two jerry cans. They then took a blanket, a tin that had held some of their provisions, a few odd pieces of clothing and the cover that had been over the top of the boat, and threw them into the sea, along with a spare oar that Fred had placed in the bottom of the boat.

Uncle Fred kept a keen check on a little compass that he had in his pocket. It was not long before the sea's current changed as they came out of the shelter of Jersey. They were now in the main open seaway of the English Channel and heading towards Guernsey.

Linda was the first to hear the 'splash, splash, splash' sound of a boat cutting through the waves at speed and rounding the north-west tip of Jersey, and heading across the top of the island towards the area where the Germans had fired at them.

"That's them," Uncle Fred exclaimed, as they saw a fast German patrol boat skimming across the water shining a beam out across its bows as it went. The three watched it as it sped east away from them and into the distance close to the towering cliffs from which they had originally intended to escape.

"It worked!" exclaimed Jerry, smiling for the first time since they had launched off the Island.

"It has so far," said Linda, with some trepidation, "but we still have a long way to go."

The next hour passed very slowly. "My friends live almost on the coast in the forest area of Guernsey," explained Uncle Fred. "I used to bring my boat and tie it up in a natural harbour below where they live, and then swim to shore and scale the cliffs." He saw the look of disbelief in the eyes of his two young companions and he added, "That was in my younger days, of course, but I'll just do it again if I have to!"

Eventually the coastline of Guernsey appeared out of the gloomy darkness. Very carefully, Uncle Fred steered the boat along the south side of the Island, keeping a safe distance from the coast so as not to be heard by any lookouts this time. Once he knew where he was, he cut the engine and started to row the boat closer into the shore. "If I start rowing here," he explained, "I shall catch the current of the sea and that should help take us in towards the shore." Uncle Fred once again very proficiently and silently pulled the boat along with the oars until they were under the towering cliffs of the south side of Guernsey.

CHAPTER 24

Guernsey

"Right," Fred said purposefully, pulling the oars out of the water and allowing the boat to drift towards the base of the cliffs. "This is where we will anchor as it's hidden from the top of the cliffs. I'll swim from here; if we go any closer the boat might be damaged."

He lowered the anchor over the side of the boat and changed down to his underclothes. "I'll swim much better in my vest and long johns," he explained. "Now, I plan to be no more than two hours at the most. Hopefully I can get up the cliffs unnoticed. When I get there, I will fill any cans I can get hold of just over half-full, so that they will float. I will throw them down into the sea near here and hopefully you can collect them and haul them into the boat. I know at my age I'll never manage to carry several cans of liquid down those cliffs." He paused to take a breath, then added, "If I am not back in two hours you must go on without me. Do you understand? It is important that you get to England. I know that you can both do it. Okay, all clear?" he asked as he prepared to drop himself over the side of the boat and into the water.

"Yes," both replied almost in unison, and then Linda added, "But you will come back, won't you?"

He looked at her earnestly, "Yes, I'll try my very best to come back, pet, you can be sure of that, but always remember that promise from God that He will be with you as you pass through the waters!" Then he let go of the side of the boat and swam away quietly towards the bottom of the cliffs. The two children watched him in admiration as he pulled himself onto a natural stone ledge at the base of the cliff. Carefully, he began a very perilous climb up the sharp and jagged cliffs until about fifty feet above the sea, where he found a natural path that seemed to rise dangerously up to the top of the cliffs. With the overhang of the rocks above the boat and the darkness of the moonless night, the two children lost sight of him once he was on the path.

It was a long and frightening wait for the two children. They sat huddled up in the boat as it bobbed restlessly up and down, listening to the ceaseless roaring of the waves crashing against the cliffs just a few yards away from them. Each minute seemed like an hour to them as they checked and rechecked their watches, whilst eagerly waiting for the return of Uncle Fred with the much-needed diesel. After about an hour and a half they heard a noise from above and strained their eyes through the darkness in the hope of catching the form of dear Uncle Fred returning down the cliff.

At last, out of the darkness they saw his outline as he came to the start of the cliff path and then they heard his familiar voice couched in a low hoarse whisper, "I've got some, I'm going to throw the cans to you from here and then climb down and join you."

"Great," echoed the children as the first metal canister landed with a splash almost alongside the boat.

"Hey," whispered Jerry as loudly as he dared, "make sure you miss us, won't you?"

The old man stood on the cliff and gave a little laugh, "Of course I will, I'll be throwing them further out over there to your right," and with that he scrambled part-way back up the cliff path. The two hurriedly pulled the heavy jerry can out of the sea into the boat, thankful that, as promised, it was only half-full. About three minutes later the children heard a splash in the distance roughly in the direction that Uncle Fred had indicated. This was followed closely by another splash, and then another. Then suddenly, through the gloom they heard the unmistakable shout of a German guard.

"Halt!" Another splash sounded from the sea. "Halt." This

time the voice sounded much louder and more authoritative. "Hände hoch! Hands up!" the voice spoke again.

Then again they heard another voice speaking in German, and then in English. "Warum sind Sie hier? Why are you here?"

The two children froze in terror! The Germans had caught Uncle Fred! Then they heard yet another splash as another can fell into the sea and, to the children's horror, they heard a single pistol shot followed by a very loud groan. Then they heard a voice that they recognised call out, "Get away! Go," and then muffled voices all talking in German.

"Oh no," whispered Jerry in disbelief. "They've shot Uncle Fred!"

"But they can't have," Linda spluttered. "They can't have."

Jerry looked up into the darkness of the cliffs, hoping that his uncle would come running down the cliff track to find them. They could still hear excited voices calling in German through the darkness, then unmistakably a voice they recognised, loud, clear and penetrating through the night, "Pass through the waters! Pass through the waters!"

"That's Uncle Fred," Jerry whispered, "and he's calling to us, he's telling us to go without him."

"But we can't," answered Linda, tears welling up in her eyes. "We can't leave him there with the Germans!"

"We have no choice," Jerry whispered, realising that any German soldier coming down that track might see them. "We must do as he said."

Linda looked across at Jerry, aghast, "We can't go now, can we?" she exclaimed. "We don't know what to do!"

"Well, first of all let's collect those cans out of the sea," replied Jerry, looking at Linda through his own tear-filled eyes. "We only need one guard to scramble down that path and see us and we'll have had it too."

"You're right." Linda suddenly realised that now the whole mission to warn the authorities of Hitler's visit to Jersey was right back on their shoulders.

"Okay," Jerry said, "I can't row the boat by myself, it's far too big, so you will have to take one side and me the other."

Working together, they managed to pull up the grappling anchor and get into position to row out. "Hey," whispered Jerry with alarm, "we are being dragged towards the cliffs."

As the boat was borne along by the current, the two tried to work the oars in unison and push out against the sea. Little by little, the boat moved away from the jagged features of the rocks along the cliff base. "There's a can," said Jerry, as his oar struck a metal object floating in the sea just off to his right. He tried to knock it several times with the oar in order to pull it closer to the boat. Eventually, with a combination of the tide and his efforts, the can floated alongside and Jerry hauled it up into the boat.

"I can't see any of the others," Linda said, as she looked round, whilst pulling hard on her oar.

"I think the tide might have carried them away," Jerry answered. Just then, he caught sight of something bobbing in the water just behind the boat. "Hey, there's another one." Both stopped rowing and let the boat drift back towards the great expanse of cliffs until they were right over the dark shape of a metal canister. Jerry scrambled to the back of the boat and leaned over, trying to get a grip of it. The cylindrical canister was a different shape to the other two, and he found it hard to get a grip but finally managed, and with a heave and a sigh brought it safely into the boat. "Wow," he said as he looked up at the cliffs towering above them, "I hope no-one shines a light down here to see us."

"I do too," replied Linda. "We are still okay, but what about Uncle Fred?"

"Well we must get to England now, for his sake," Jerry replied. "If his call was for us to go away we had better do as he said. Whatever has happened to him we need to be brave. I just hope that he is okay. His last call about 'passing through the waters' sounded strong enough, maybe the shot we heard only gave him a flesh wound."

"Let's hope so," said Linda, still pulling hard on the oar, then she added, "Hey, let's pray too; you know how Uncle Fred believes in God and told us how God had saved him when he missed his boat in Belfast. Why don't we ask God to save him again?"

"Yes, that's a great idea," Jerry answered, as they carried on rowing the boat. "But how should we pray?"

"Well, your uncle prayed out loud when he thanked God for the food before we left," Linda answered.

"Oh, I couldn't pray out loud!" Jerry exclaimed, "I'd be so embarrassed and wouldn't know what to say."

"Well, maybe we can both pray for Uncle Fred silently as we row?"

"Yes, okay, I don't mind that."

They continued rowing, speaking silently to God. They asked Him to take care of Uncle Fred who had done so much to help them in their vital mission.

After what seemed to both a long time of prayer, Linda said, "Didn't your uncle put a Bible in his box of essentials? Let's look and see if we can read something from it. If God could speak to your uncle from it, then maybe He will speak to us too."

"Okay, we'll have a look," Jerry said enthusiastically, "but first we need to get away from here; it's still too dangerous. Come on!" he said stoically, "We still have a long way to go and an important mission to accomplish."

CHAPTER 25

Into The Channel

They were glad to pull around the bay away from danger, however having to leave Uncle Fred to his fate tore at their insides. Both Jerry and Linda now knew that the sound of the sea rolling up against the rock face would drown any noise they were making with the oars. What an excellent job Uncle Fred had done as he had rowed them away from Jersey. They were finding the rowing hard going, and trying to keep both oars working together was proving very difficult. Eventually they decided they were far enough out to sea to start the engine once again. Jerry, knowing that Linda was by far the better mechanic, handed that job over to her. She checked the amount of fuel remaining and then filled up the tank from the containers. Then she carefully bled the airline and primed the engine before pulling the starter cord. The engine coughed and spluttered, and then died away. Carefully Linda went through the procedure again, bleeding the air and priming the engine with fuel. She yanked the cord and again the engine turned over, spluttering and shuddering as it tried to spring into life. Eventually, the engine caught and it roared into full power. Jerry was so relieved that, forgetting they were still very close to Guernsey, he called out, "Yippee," rather too loudly.

"Stupid!" said Linda irritably. "Do you want to get us caught as well?"

"Oh, sorry," replied a rather chastised Jerry. "I forgot."

"Oh, well," replied his companion. "You had better take control of the tiller and start steering us." Jerry took hold of the boat's tiller and began to steer, turning towards the west, and thus avoiding going up the east side where the main harbour of St. Peter Port lay along with a number of smaller islands all held by the German forces.

"It's a good job that Uncle Fred told us to sail this way because I might have tried to go out past Herm and then we'd have been sitting ducks for any German patrols," he told Linda. Then he added," I hope that we still have my uncle's compass here."

"Where did he leave it?" Linda searched through Uncle Fred's jacket pockets and then triumphantly pulled out a metal compass and passed it to her friend.

"Great," he said. "I guess that now we've passed the southwest point of the Island, if we steer due north we should eventually reach the coast of England, and hopefully we'll not end up in the Atlantic Ocean." He thought carefully and then added, "Still, the coast of England extends a long way down to Cornwall from what I remember from my geography lessons, so hopefully as long as we keep going north we should land somewhere on the south coast of England."

"But," interjected Linda, with an anxious edge to her voice, "what about the fuel? Do you think we will have enough to get all that way? After all, it's nearly a hundred miles."

"I don't know," replied Jerry, frowning. "Anyway, you are the mechanic; you should know that better than me. I only know that we must get as far up the Channel as we can and away from these Islands by daybreak. The closer to England we get the closer we are to safety, so we must keep the motor running as long as we can.

"Now what I reckon is that we both need some sleep. I am exhausted, so we will take turns of one hour shifts to keep watch and steer, whilst the other rests. I suggest you sleep first and I'll keep us on course for the first hour."

"But before we do that we must read your uncle's Bible," Linda said as she slipped off her wooden seat and opened the wooden box that contained the precious little Book. "Here it is," she said confidently, as she lifted it out and sat back on her seat.

It was difficult to read in the darkness of the night, but by changing positions Linda managed to get just enough light from the moon and stars to see the book as she opened it up. "Hey, look!" she gasped as she opened its pages. "There's a bookmark here in these pages; someone has underlined this part in pen."

"Can you make out what it says?" Jerry asked, as he kept one hand on the boat's tiller and the other holding tightly to the compass.

"I think so," Linda said, as she strained to read the words in the darkness. "It says, 'Let not your heart be troubled: ye believe in God, believe also in me', then there is a gap before a bit more is underlined which says, 'How can we know the way? Jesus saith unto him, I am the way, the truth, and the life: no man cometh unto the Father, but by me.' How strange!"

She looked up from the book, her eyes relaxing as she stopped straining to read the words. "Whatever does that mean?"

Jerry thought out loud, "Firstly, I think maybe my uncle underlined those words and placed that bookmark there, just in case something happened to him, so that we would find them and read them."

"Do you really think so?" asked Linda in amazement.

"Yes, I do. What was the first bit about not letting your heart be troubled? I think that's to tell us not to worry, because everything will work out in the end."

"Um, I'm not so sure," Linda answered, as she again strained to read the words.

"Then didn't it say something like 'How can we know the way?' Well, that's just what we need to know - the way to go."

"Well, I think we should read it again in the morning when I am not so tired. It's all too much for me to understand at the moment." Then she sighed, "I just hope that the Germans are nice to Uncle Fred."

"Yes, so do I. So do I," replied Jerry slowly.

It did not take Linda long to snuggle down among the blankets and the clothes that festooned the bottom of the boat. Even despite the momentous events of the night and the great sorrow that she felt in not knowing what had happened to Jerry's uncle, the continual droning of the engine and the gentle splashing of the sea as the boat's bow glided through the water soon sent her off into a deep and much needed sleep.

Linda woke with a start to see the sun quite high in the mid-summer sky. It took her a while to come to her senses and realise just where she was, and remember the events of the previous night. She realised that the engine had stopped and looked back to see Jerry slumped over the tiller, sound asleep.

"Jerry, Jerry!" she called in a wild panic. "Wake up, wake up!"

"What's the matter?" Jerry stirred and groaned as he slowly opened his eyes, but quickly shut them again at the bright glare of the sunlight.

"Jerry," Linda called again. "Where are we?"

Jerry shook his head as if trying to get himself back into the real world, then he looked about him. "Oh, no," he gasped. "I guess I must have fallen asleep. What time is it?"

Linda looked at her little watch and said, "Seven-thirty, near enough. But when did you fall asleep?" she asked with great anxiety in her voice.

"I don't know," replied Jerry, with a sort of faraway look in his eyes. "I remember you going to sleep, but little else after that. Oh, Linda," he groaned, "we could have drifted miles off course whilst I have been sleeping. I should have been looking out and keeping us on course. Oh, how foolish and stupid of me!"

"Well," said Linda, taking a big gulp of air and swallowing hard, "let's think now. I guess it was about four to four-thirty that I went to sleep and so let's say we both slept for three hours. That engine should have run for at least two hours before it ran out of fuel, but with you asleep we could have been going round in circles and wasting all that precious diesel. Oh, Jerry, what are we going to do?"

"I might have been steering us right out into the Atlantic Ocean," Jerry replied. "Oh, Linda, I am so very sorry." There was silence as the two looked out to sea in all directions hoping to see some sign of land, some landmark that might give them a clue as to their whereabouts; but there was nothing as far as the eye could see, except the vast blue and green expanse of water. Jerry picked up the compass, which had fallen from his hand and was lying on top of a bag in the bottom of the boat. "It shows that north is across there," he said, pointing to his right.

"That means we have been heading out west and into the Atlantic, and if we have been on this course since you fell asleep then I really have no idea how far we have travelled or which way to go," she added seriously.

"I have an idea," said Jerry, deeply distressed that his own inability to keep awake had got them into this predicament. "If we refill the tank and then start the engine and keep heading north-east that should bring us somewhere near land, either back to the Channel Islands if we have drifted too far south, or if not back up towards the English coast. Anyway, it's our only option. What we have to hope for is that there will be enough fuel to get us near enough to England to be seen and get help. Come on, let's stop worrying and get going!"

Once more, Linda screwed open the metal top to the engine's fuel tank and, with Jerry's help, emptied the contents of one of the containers into it. Once the tank was full, Linda adjusted the air intake valve and primed the engine, allowing some of the fuel to flow into the starting chamber. She pulled the engine cord and there was a crack and a cough, but then nothing. Again, she primed the tank and pulled the cord. Again, the engine cracked and coughed, and then died away. "I think some dirt from the bottom of the tank may have clogged up the system," she explained to a frustrated and exasperated Jerry. "I'll have to undo this fuel line and let the diesel run out. If the engine still will not start, then I will have to check on the main fuel cylinder. Linda took the fuel line off the engine, and putting it to her lips she sucked hard and then spat out the contents. She then took a mouthful of water from one of the water bottles they had brought and rinsed out her mouth. "Yuk," she shuddered, "I hate doing jobs like that but sometimes suction is the only way to get the fuel to flow if priming does not work. Now let's reattach this and see what happens." She took a screwdriver and re-attached the fuel line to the main engine. Then carefully setting the priming arm once again to allow the fuel to flow she pulled the starting cord. This time there was a crack, a cough and a splutter and then the engine purred into life.

"Oh, wonderful!" exclaimed Jerry. "Linda, you're a genius!"

"Not really," she answered modestly. "It's just that living on a farm I have watched Dad with our old tractor and learned from him. Anyway, let's start going north-east as fast as we can and we'll both keep a lookout this time."

CHAPTER 26

Wind Power

The engine purred monotonously as the little craft made its way slowly across the English Channel; hopefully towards England! Jerry pulled out the plans of the German fortifications and troop concentrations, given to him by the Bailiff of the Island, and studied them carefully. "So much," mused Jerry, "rests on us being able to get to England."

"Will you read those verses from the Bible again, please?" he requested, after about an hour.

Linda picked up the worn, black Bible and opened it where the bookmark was placed and again read, 'Let not your heart be troubled: ye believe in God, believe also in Me. How can we know the way? Jesus saith unto him, I am the way, the truth, and the life: no man cometh unto the Father, but by Me.'

Jerry looked up into the sky, "I wonder if God really is speaking to us in those words."

"How do you mean?" Linda quizzed.

"Well, He's telling us not to be troubled and that He is the way."

"You mean it's a bit like a code that we have to work out," Linda added, leaning forward on her seat, staring at the open Bible in her hand.

"Well, not so much like a code, but more a promise from God to us."

"Like that one Uncle Fred read to us yesterday about passing through the waters?"

"Yes, something like that," replied Jerry with a frown.

"I think I've got it," Linda said, suddenly looking up and staring at Jerry.

"Got what?"

"What this means. Look," she said, holding up the Bible, "Jesus said these words, and He said not only were we to believe in God, but in Him too. Then He said He was the way... to the Father. Don't you see it, Jerry?" She looked anxiously across the boat.

"See what?" he asked, looking at her in a perplexed way.

"Well, God the Father lives in heaven and Jesus was saying that He was the way there. He said it was not just enough to believe in God. We need to believe in Him as well. Don't you remember your uncle speaking about trusting Jesus as his Saviour?"

"You mean that time he told us about, when he was in Belfast and he became a Christian?"

"Yes, that's just what I mean," Linda said with a smile. "He said he'd trusted Jesus to save him."

"You mean he'd asked the *Lord* Jesus to save him," Jerry corrected. "Uncle Fred always calls Him the Lord Jesus."

"Okay, the *Lord* Jesus," Linda replied. "Well, I think that these verses Uncle Fred bookmarked are possibly a promise, as you said, telling us not to let our hearts be troubled, and also showing that God is the way, but do you not think these verses are really telling us it is only by trusting in the Lord Jesus that we can get to heaven?"

"I think you're maybe right there," Jerry agreed. "I had never really thought of it like that before. Ummm, if that's the case, then this is a serious thing because it involves us, God and the Lord Jesus, so I think we should both think about this a bit more."

After about another hour, the engine began to splutter. "Quick," said Linda, "stop it now, before it drags some dirt into it and I have to clean out the various parts again."

Jerry, who was holding the tiller, flicked the little throttle switch from 'On' to 'Idle' and then across to 'Stop' and the engine died away.

"We need to refill the tank," Linda said as she lifted one of the diesel containers across to Jerry. "Not much left in this one," she said as she handed it to him.

"No," agreed Jerry. He unscrewed the top and commenced pouring the contents into the engine's tank. The diesel was soon exhausted and Jerry threw the empty can overboard almost in disgust.

"You shouldn't have done that," Linda scolded. "Remember what your uncle did last night to try and make the Germans think that we had been hit by their gunfire and sunk? We must keep anything we can in case we need to try that trick again."

"You're right," answered Jerry, as he watched the container rapidly floating away in front of the boat. "Hey!" he shouted. "Look at which way that container has gone! That means the current is going in our direction. I threw it out at the back, and it has been swept around in front of us. That's a great help as the current will hopefully take us in the direction we want to go." With that, he took the last of the diesel containers and poured its contents into the fuel tank. Then, exchanging places with Linda, he watched again as she carefully primed the engine and pulled the starting cord. There was a bang and a splutter and then once again the engine started.

"Great," said Jerry, checking his compass once again. "North by east it is."

"Aye, aye, Captain," Linda said with a giggle as Jerry once again took control of the tiller.

Jerry laughed and then said, "You know that is the first time we have smiled since yesterday!" The two looked across the boat at each other and then burst into spontaneous laughter as all the pent-up strain and stress of the last twenty-four hours erupted in one continuous peel of mirth. "Oh," said Jerry after calming down a little, "the captain is hungry and needs some food."

"On its way, sir," Linda saluted as she dug into the various boxes and bags that their parents had given them. As she passed some bread and cheese across to Jerry, she said, "Do you know, Jerry, we have not eaten since tea last night?"

"No, I guess not," replied Jerry, "but I haven't felt much like eating 'cause my stomach was all knotted up until now."

With bread, cheese, some raw vegetables and fruit the two children made short work of the food that Linda had chosen for their meal. She said, "Oh well, I guess we have enough stuff here for four more meals if we need them and there is plenty of water in these bottles, so hopefully we should be okay as long as we are not too far away from land."

"I hope we aren't," answered Jerry. "I really hope we aren't."

It was about an hour after they had finished their meal that it happened. Both of them were just thinking that they were making excellent progress through the vast expanse of sea before them when, suddenly, the engine started to make some very unusual choking noises. These noises were rapidly followed by three or four large bangs which shook the small boat, bringing anxious cries from the children before the engine finally cut out with a gurgle and a hiss.

"What's happened?" wailed Jerry, as the boat slowed and began to gently rock.

"I don't know," replied Linda, with a worried frown on her face. "It doesn't sound great, does it?" Quickly, she moved across to the engine and began to examine it. "Well, there is still fuel," she exclaimed, "and I can't see any blockage in the fuel line. It sounded like the bearings inside, but they shouldn't have gone just like that, unless...Jerry, help me lift the engine out of the water." Together they undid the two clasp fixings and hauled on the engine, but it would not pivot on its anchor point to allow the propeller blades to come free of the water.

"What's stopping it?" asked Jerry worriedly.

"I think that something must have fouled up the propeller, which has caused the engine to strain and ruin the bearings. Whatever it is, it's caught on the propeller and won't allow us to lift the engine clear. Let's try one last time." They both heaved and the engine gave, but only a little, before they had to release it and let it drop back into its rest. "Well," Linda suggested, "one of us will have to get into the water and feel around to see if we can dislodge whatever it is that's caught on the propeller or else we just detach the engine here and let it drop off the boat."

"Okay," said Jerry, "I'll go, just don't go trying to start the engine whilst I am down there."

"Don't worry, I won't," replied Linda, with a forced laugh in her voice. Jerry carefully took off his shoes and socks, his coat and his jersey before gingerly lowering himself over the back of the boat. He shivered as he entered the freezing water, then groped around with his hands below the water level and exclaimed, "I can feel something like rope all caught up around the propeller blades. There is so much of it that I can't even feel the propeller."

He dived under the boat, and then surfaced, grabbing at the side whilst at the same time wiping the salt water out of his eyes. "Linda," he said, "there's loads of it all under the boat; I don't think I will be able to free it, not without a knife anyway."

Linda looked around her, "Do we have one?"

"I think so," replied Jerry as he pulled himself up on the side of the boat and peered into it. "I seem to remember Mum giving us Dad's old penknife with the other bits and pieces they collected for us." As quickly, and carefully as she could, Linda worked her way through the various necessities that they had brought with them for the journey, searching for an all-important knife.

"Here," she squealed triumphantly as she produced the penknife from one of the potato sacks. "Will this do?"

Jerry looked at it with a frown. "It looks very small but as it's all we have it will be better than nothing anyway. I'll do the best I can."

Linda opened out the blade of the penknife, which was about three inches long, and handed it, handle first, to Jerry. "Be careful," she advised, as he took the knife and swam round to the stern of the boat.

"I will," he answered as he took a deep breath before diving under the water. Linda peered anxiously over the back of the boat and watched Jerry as he worked away just below the surface, trying to cut the rope free from the propeller blades. He came up for air time after time. "Wow," he spluttered as he came up on one occasion, "there is just so much of it and it's so thick and heavy that it seems I'll never be able to do it."

"Keep trying," Linda encouraged.

After several more deep breaths and underwater dives, Jerry surfaced again with a triumphant cry, "I've done it! That's it, all free!"

He pulled himself up on the side of the boat and Linda helped haul him in. He flopped into the hull and lay there gasping and shivering, "I think it must have been some kind of rope floating just below the surface, possibly thrown overboard from an old fishing boat," he spluttered. "It was very long and covered in seaweed and other things and it was totally wrapped around the propellers and the drive shaft."

Linda handed Jerry a towel and said, "Well, let's just hope it's not caused the engine any real damage." Jerry moved out of her way as she once more primed the engine and pulled the starting cord. The engine made a loud bang and shuddered. Then picking up a bit it shook violently, making an awful noise and causing the whole boat to tremble. Linda squatted down and held onto the side to stop herself overbalancing and falling into the sea. "I think," she shouted, "that the bearings have gone!"

"What did you say?" yelled Jerry above the din.

"I said that I think the bearings have gone." She pushed the little switch over to 'Idle' and then 'Stop' and the noise and vibration ceased. "It's the bearings," Linda told him again. "They have gone and since we don't move forward when the engine is going, I don't think the drive shaft is connecting either."

"Well," asked Jerry, "what can we do about it?"

"Nothing," Linda responded. "The engine is completely broken and useless."

"So," replied Jerry, "I guess this is where the spare engine comes in handy! We need to change the two engines over, don't we?"

"Well, yes," answered Linda very hesitantly. "The only problem is that there's so little fuel left that it would be a waste of time swapping them." Linda paused. "I think the best thing to do is detach the engine and let it drop off the boat. Then we can use the sail and try to tack up the Channel to land. I know it will be hard work but it may be our only option."

They both contemplated the situation for a while, before Jerry decided rather reluctantly, "I guess you're right."

"Come on then," said Linda. "Let's get this old engine undone."

It took the two of them about fifteen minutes to undo the fixing mounts on the engine and lift it out of its bracket to drop it down into its last resting place in the murky depths of the English Channel. With the weight of the engine gone, the boat seemed to rock more freely on the water, and both felt that every ripple and swell might tip them out of the boat at any moment. They picked up the crude sail and mast that Uncle Fred had made and dropped it into the socket in the bottom of the boat. Jerry took the tiller whilst Linda took the rope at the edge of the sail. The wind filled the sail and the boat pitched a little, but it began to make its way across the sea. "England, here we come!" shouted Linda optimistically.

CHAPTER 27

Land Ahoy

Both children were soon exhausted. Linda's hand ached from straining against the sail as it caught the breeze and carried the boat along. Regularly the two swapped places in order to give each other a rest. The boat cut a zigzag pattern through the water as they swung the sail, first to the port side and then to the starboard side, in an endeavour to bear north-east, as guided by the compass. Both hoped and prayed that they were heading in the right direction and that land would soon be in sight.

Jerry was the first to realise that the sun was now sinking rapidly behind them in the west, and that soon nightfall would be upon them. "We can't afford to allow ourselves to go to sleep again," he said, voicing his thoughts out loud, as the boat once again tacked round to keep on course.

"Yes," added Linda earnestly, "if we do we might never see land again!"

"Well, we seem to be making good progress even if we don't really know where we are. At least both the wind and the sea are with us and the sea is not too rough, which is such a help."

"I just hope," added Linda, "that we don't encounter any ships during the night, because they would never see us if we were in their path."

Jerry added, "Yes, but even if they did see us we would have no idea if they were British or German boats, would we?" Both stopped to look back at the beautiful view of the sun dropping down over the horizon.

"Come on," said Jerry. "I'm hungry and thirsty; let's have something more to eat."

The cold night air suddenly hit the two of them as soon as the sun sank down below the horizon. The gathering gloom made looking for any sign of land or ships in the distance virtually impossible, still their boat skipped across the dark waters of the English Channel. What they would do when they reached England and how they were going to get their vital message to the right people, they hadn't a clue. All they knew for now was that they had to get to England no matter what happened. They both just prayed hard that the wind would not die down and that the sea currents would not change. They huddled into their blankets, thankful that at least it was a clear night. Their boat continued to tack back and forth as the boom on the homemade sail continually caught the stiffening breeze.

"I think the wind is getting up," Jerry said, as he pulled the blanket tighter around him.

"Yes, I was just thinking that myself," replied Linda, keeping a tight hold on the boom as the wind grabbed at the sail and tried to tear it from her grasp. "The sea is becoming rougher too. In fact, I think I feel a bit seasick," she groaned.

"Just as long as that wind doesn't change direction or become too rough and swamp the boat, we should be okay," Jerry replied.

The boat began to pitch up and down vigorously on the swell as it made its way through the night, on a now very choppy sea. Unable to see anything in the darkness, the journey seemed to continue endlessly but the two exhausted children continued to work hard. Gradually the weather became squally and large raindrops began to fall.

"Oh, no!" exclaimed Jerry with alarm. "That's all we need; a stronger wind, a choppy sea and now the rain to soak us through." As the rain began to intensify he felt like crying. He hadn't cried for a long time. Biting his lip he tried to remember back to when he last had cried. Oh yes, it was when he had tripped over a rock submerged under the sea whilst crossing between Le Quaisné and St. Brelade's Bay a couple of years ago. He had cut himself very badly and still had a small scar on his knee to prove it. But this, he reasoned with himself, was worse than that – much, much worse! Back then his mum had bathed the knee and bandaged it up, but now he and his friend were alone and lost in an open boat with a storm apparently about to erupt in all its fury upon them. He thought of his parents back home in their beautiful granite farmhouse in St. Lawrence and longed to be there in the warmth with them, around the roaring log fire. He though of his Uncle Fred - was he still alive? Had he been shot? Would the Germans torture him to find out what he was doing? Would they then extradite him to Germany or execute him?

"Oh, if only we hadn't come," he called out, to no one in particular.

"Hush," said Linda, with the air of someone who had just made a world-shattering discovery. "Listen," she called, above the ever-increasing noise of the wind, sea and rain.

What can you hear?" Jerry sought to pull himself out of his dark and brooding thoughts and listened hard.

"Waves!" she exclaimed. "I can hear waves breaking on the shore!"

He paused to listen again. "There must be land over there!" he exclaimed as he pointed in the direction from which the sound seemed to come. "We need to change course slightly," he said, "and head more to the north than the east."

Linda changed tack on the sail again and Jerry pulled hard on the tiller to bring the little boat around. "Yes, that is the sound of waves crashing!" shouted Linda, excitedly fighting to keep the sail into the wind. "We're near land! Oh, Jerry, we are near land, we have made it!"

Carefully, Jerry set a course in the direction of the sound of the breaking waves, while Linda concentrated on keeping the sail into the wind. Suddenly Jerry saw a large, dark shape rising up out of the sea almost straight in front of them. Linda saw it almost at the same time and screamed a warning, "Jerry, look out!" But it was too late! The wind in the sail and the force of the incoming tide caught up the boat and carried it straight into a large rock with such force that it flung both Jerry and Linda into the bottom of the boat. Then, before they had time to pick themselves up, another wave lashed the boat and swung the stern around, carrying the boat past the rock and sideways on into another projection.

"We're on the rocks," called Jerry. "We'll be smashed to pieces unless we do something." As he spoke, another wave came crashing over the boat, filling it with icy cold seawater and soaking the children.

Linda gasped from the cold and tried to pick herself up. Another wave bore down on the fragile craft and picked it up in all its force, flinging it stern first against yet another large, dark shape that rose eerily out of the foaming water.

"We'll be smashed to pieces," shouted Jerry again above the roar of the wind and waves. "No wonder we could hear the breakers out there." Then through the eerie darkness Jerry caught sight of something that made his heart freeze in horror. "Cliffs!" he called out in terror, trying to point in the direction of the imposing rock face which seemed to rise out of the stormy sea. "Cliffs," he again shouted out. "We're under some mighty white cliffs."

At that point, another wave struck the boat and the two children were flung like rag dolls out of the small boat and into the seething surf. They coughed and spluttered as wave after wave crashed over them, trying desperately to swim through the sea and pull themselves onto the rocks that surrounded them.

Suddenly, Linda called out in an exhausted voice, "Sand, I can feel sand!" Jerry, who only just heard her through the crashing of the surf, stopped swimming and placed his feet on the bottom of the sea. He could feel the sand under his feet too. As he tried to stand up, he looked back and saw the remains of their boat being carried on a wave heading in his direction. Jerry just had time to duck and cover his head before everything went black and silence descended upon him.

CHAPTER 28

Washed Up

"Jerry! Jerry!" Linda cried again to the seemingly lifeless figure whose head she held in her lap. She was sat on the wet sand oblivious to the breakers crashing in front of her and the wind that still blew around her. "Jerry! Oh, Jerry, do wake up." Very slowly, Jerry turned his head and looked up groggily towards his friend. "Oh, Jerry, I thought you were dead," cried Linda with tears running down her cheeks. Jerry turned his face away and with his right hand felt for his head, which ached painfully. As he placed his hand against his temple, he felt something sticky in his hair and pulling his hand in front of his face, he carefully inspected the red substance that now covered his hand.

"Am I badly cut?" he managed to stammer, his whole body shaking with the cold and the shock.

"You have a bad gash on the top of your head," Linda answered, trying to remain as calm as possible, "but I think you'll be okay. Some part of the boat hit you after we were thrown out into the sea."

"How did I get here on to the beach?" asked Jerry, holding his head and letting out a slight moan.

"I dragged you," replied Linda simply.

"Thank you, Linda. I guess you saved my life," he said to his friend as he tried to lift his head.

"Maybe," Linda answered, "but it wasn't far and it's not much of a beach with so many of these stones." She dug her heels into the shale stones she was sitting on and asked, "Where do you think we are, Jerry? Do you think that this is England?"

Jerry, rubbing his head and trying hard to clear his foggy mind replied, "I don't know. It may be that we missed England completely and have gone right back across the Channel to France." He paused as he tried to think through the pain that numbed his body, "There is only one way to find out, I guess, and that's to get off this beach and find some civilisation." He tried to roll his head off Linda's lap and get up. He waited, positioned on all fours, before trying to stand up. He was halfway up when suddenly he felt as if his head was being hit with a sledgehammer, and he fell back down with a thud.

"Jerry," Linda cried, as he lay motionless on the ground once again. Her tears mingled with the rain as she tried to talk to him.

After a few very long seconds Jerry spoke. "I guess I am not as strong as I thought I was."

"Oh, you'll be fine," said Linda, trying to sound as brave as she could. "I'm sure this is England and soon we'll be able to tell them just why we've come."

Jerry smiled and closed his eyes. "Jerry," she called, "I need you to help me. We must move a little further up the beach and get some shelter from those cliffs and then wait until daylight." She got no response so she repeated herself as loud as she could above the crashing waves. "We must get some shelter and you'll have to help me move you up the beach."

"I know," Jerry replied feebly.

"It's not far," Linda continued, as she looked up the beach into the darkness, "but I don't think that I am strong enough to carry you up there myself, but if you can try to get on your feet I can help you."

"Okay," Jerry answered in a far away voice, "I'll do my best."

Linda carefully placed Jerry's head back on the sand and got up. She bent down and took his hands and asked, "Are you ready?"

Jerry managed to get himself on to all fours again and, very slowly, Linda helped him to stand up. With one arm over Linda's shoulder and the other supporting his head, they managed little by little to move up the beach away from the crashing waves and towards the shelter of the looming cliffs. It took them several minutes to cover the few feet from the water's edge to the cliffs, but to the soaking wet children in pitch darkness it seemed like an eternity. Eventually, Linda fell exhausted next to Jerry. She was shivering, as much from fear as from the intense cold she felt from her wet clothes and the wind and rain. "Curl up under here," she told Jerry, as she found a crevice in the rock where they could both get some shelter. "I'm going back to see if I can salvage anything from the remains of the boat."

Linda headed back down the beach towards the sea, while Jerry sat huddled up, shivering and longing to be able to change into warm, dry clothes. Soon he heard Linda coming slowly back up the beach. She was pulling a large piece of the boat behind her. "Nothing much that I can see is left," she said as she drew nearer, "but hopefully this will make some kind of a shelter for us." Then, with what strength she had left, she pushed the wood up against the cliff face making a kind of covered shelter over Jerry. "It's not much," she confessed, "but it will at least keep some of the rain off." She readjusted the wood and then crawled in next to her companion. "Well, at least the tide has turned," she said as she sat down in her wet clothes. "I was worried that it might come right up to these cliffs and drown us."

Jerry smiled weakly through the pain. It was just like Linda to think of the worst scenario and be prepared for it! He knew that not many girls would have had the courage to embark on the adventure that they had set out on. With these thoughts passing through his aching head, he fell into a fitful sleep.

The sun was quite high in the sky when Linda finally awoke. She opened her eyes to find its warm rays shining through the rough shelter. Still feeling damp and rather stiff she stretched herself out and then crawled out of the shelter to find herself on a pebbly beach with the white cliffs towering high above her head. She pulled herself back into the shelter and called softly, "Jerry! Wake up!" He gave a groan and rolled over. "Jerry, we need to be going."

Jerry opened his eyes and asked wearily, "Where are we?"

"I am not sure yet," Linda answered truthfully. "Hopefully somewhere on the south coast of England."

Jerry groaned again as the memory of the previous night's events came to him. He remembered the crashing surf, the unmanageable boat, the rocks, the waves, being thrown out of the boat, and then seeing part of the boat coming straight for him! He reached up and felt his head. He could feel his matted hair full of sand but was relieved to find that, as far as he could tell, the bleeding had stopped. Carefully and very slowly, he crawled out of the shelter and tried to stand up. As he did so, the pain shot through his head again and he slumped to the ground. Linda caught him and helped him to his feet. With some effort, he managed to get up on to both feet and stood leaning against the shelter. "Right," he said more confidently than he felt, "which way will we go?"

Linda looked along the cliffs in both directions; she was amazed at both the height and the whiteness of the impregnable wall of rock that stretched along the vast expanse of coastline. *Could these be the White Cliffs of Dover?* she wondered.

"I vote that we go this way," she suggested, pointing towards where the cliffs seemed to disappear in the distance. "At least the sea seems to be away from the base of these cliffs, whereas if we go in the other direction it seems to hit the base of the cliffs further along."

"You know what," said Jerry, "I was thinking in the boat last night, just before we hit the rocks, about those verses we had read in the Bible. I think you were right about the Lord Jesus being the way to heaven, because if He isn't, why did He die on the cross?"

"Jerry," Linda interrupted, "you're injured, we are both lost and cold and all you can talk about is what we read in the Bible yesterday!"

"Yes, Linda," Jerry replied, holding his aching head and trying to steady his shaking knees. "This is important, very important, because if this is England, then God has kept the promise He made to Uncle Fred and has brought us through the waters. If that's the case then surely He expects us to trust His Son, just as Uncle Fred did in Belfast all those years ago."

"Well, maybe you're right," Linda agreed, "but let's see if this is England first!"

"Okay," said Jerry, "let's go." The two friends made their way slowly along the beach, Linda trying to support the rather unsteady Jerry.

Despite the warmth of the early morning sun the beach seemed cold and lifeless, and the cliffs, although a chalky white, appeared almost unfriendly. An occasional freestanding stack of rock appeared, making an eerie sight on the dreary beach. After about a half hour of walking at a snail's pace they came around a corner and saw, to their great joy, a large bay sweeping in front of them, with the cliffs sloping down from their dizzy heights to a little slipway in the distance. "Come on," Linda encouraged, "we are almost safe."

CHAPTER 29

Isle Of Wight

As they made their way towards the slipway, Linda caught sight of some movement halfway down another towering white cliff across the bay, beyond the slipway. "Hey, look, Jerry!" she called excitedly. "There's a man up on that cliff standing near some sort of tunnel waving at us."

Jerry pulled himself up on Linda's shoulder and tried to focus on the figure they could see running down the cliff path towards the slipway, waving frantically at them.

"Stop!" the man shouted anxiously from the slip-way as the two approached it from about two hundred yards away. The children turned to look at him. "Stop! Stop! Don't move!" he shouted again, with great urgency. "Mines! Mines! The beach is mined!"

The two children stopped dead as the importance of what they had just heard sank in. "Don't move!" As he came running along the cliffs in their direction they could see he was wearing a green uniform. He stopped above them and called again, "You two, whatever you do, don't move until help comes. There are mines on that beach, do you understand?"

Linda, who was still supporting Jerry, called back, "Y-Yes, we understand, but my friend is badly hurt."

The man on the cliffs replied, almost in a voice of exasperation, "He'll not be hurt much longer if you carry on along that beach. You'll both be dead!" Jerry and Linda remained absolutely still as the man spoke to them.

"Where are we?" Linda called, realising for the first time how thankful she was to hear an English-speaking voice.

"What do you mean?" the voice called back.

"Where are we?" Linda asked again.

"Where are you?" the man repeated from the cliffs. "Freshwater Bay! Didn't you know?"

"No," Linda called back. "Where is Freshwater Bay?"

The man on the cliffs called, "What do you mean? Are you having me on?"

"No," Linda called back across the beach to where the man stood on the cliffs about fifty feet away from them, "we've come from Jersey."

"Jersey!" The man looked up at the sky, and then said disbelievingly and with a sarcastic tone, "I guess you swam here, did you?"

"No," Linda retorted. "We came in a boat but it was wrecked when we hit some rocks around there last night," she said, pointing in the direction they had come. "That's how my friend was injured."

The man looked out along the cliffs in the direction Linda was pointing, and said, "Never! You'd never have come round that corner without blowing yourselves to bits, and apart from that, this is one of very few occasions the sea ever goes out far enough to allow you to walk along the bottom of those cliffs!"

"Well, we have," Linda called back indignantly, "and we did sail up here from Jersey."

"Well, that's..." the man started, but stopped as two more men came into view.

One, Linda could see, was wearing a peaked cap. He called out to Jerry and Linda, who were standing as still as possible on the wet sand, "Don't move, I'll have someone make a clear way for you in a minute or two." Then, looking along the cliffs from the direction they had walked, he asked, "Where have you come from?"

Linda was by now becoming not only exasperated at all the questions but also weary of supporting Jerry on her shoulder. "Jersey!" she called back and then, as if to pre-empt the next question, added, "We came in a boat and would like to know where we are."

There was a stunned silence on the cliffs as the three men looked at each other, then the man in the peaked cap answered simply, "You're on the Isle of Wight!"

"Hurray!" Linda shouted. "Hurray! We made it." As she spoke these words Jerry's limp body fell off her shoulder in a dead faint. The three on the cliffs held their breath as they saw him fall to the sand. Again the men called out, "Don't move! Whatever you do, don't move a muscle! We'll be with you as soon as we can get a sapper to check the beach and make a safe passage for you!"

As the watchers on the cliff top sprang into action, Linda knelt down next to Jerry. Carefully, she moved Jerry's damp and blood-matted hair back away from the large gash on his forehead. Then she spoke in a soft but clear and serious voice, "Jerry, Jerry, we made it," trying with all her might to rouse him from his enforced slumber. As she looked down at him, tears started to well up in her eyes and drop down her cheeks.

"We won't be long," one of the soldiers called.

Slowly and carefully, a soldier walked down onto the beach carrying a long metal-handled contraption with a ring on one end, which he hovered above the sand. Just behind this contraption, and attached to the man, was a large semi-circular shield that went almost from his feet right up to his chin. Slowly, very slowly, the soldier made his way across the damp sand. Another soldier followed on behind. He was placing marker posts in position to enable them all to find their way back safely. The young soldier with the metal pole seemed to take forever, as he wended his way across the beach towards them. Leaving a trail of marker posts behind him, he reached Linda who was still squatting on her hands and knees next to the unconscious Jerry. As the sapper drew alongside, a buzzer on his metal probe sounded, making Linda jump involuntarily with shock.

With a look of alarm, the soldier spoke to Linda from behind his protective shield. "Whatever you do, young miss, do not move your feet or your friend's body; there is a mine right next to you!" Linda froze, more in fear than in response to the command of the man who held the metal pole. Carefully and very cautiously the soldier moved around the two of them in a small circle. "Okay," he said in a calm but authoritative voice, while still holding his protective shield. "I think that the mine is right behind your friend's body. I guess it will be easier to move the mine first before moving him. What I need you to do is to make sure he does not move an inch, or it will be curtains for all of us!" Then deepening his voice to add a note of seriousness, he said, "Do you understand?"

"Yes, I do," she replied in a frightened whisper. "I'll do my very best."

Linda watched the soldier carefully remove his protective shield and place it cautiously on the sand next to them. Then, taking a knife, he scratched about in the sand behind Jerry's limp body. After a couple of minutes, the soldier said, with a note of triumph in his voice, "Found it!" He began to dig down into the sand right behind the small of Jerry's back so that he would be able to lift the mine out of the way. Just as he seemed to have it almost free Jerry let out a big groan, and stretching his body he tried to open his eyes. "Don't let him move!" the soldier called with alarm, as Jerry started to shuffle his body on the sand.

"Stay still, Jerry! Stay still!" cried Linda urgently, as she tried to hold his body away from the hole the soldier had dug around the mine behind him. Jerry opened his eyes fully and looked at her wide-eyed and frightened, as he realised that someone else was now with them.

"Where are we?" he mumbled as again he tried to reposition his aching body on the wet sand.

"Stay still!" the soldier called. "Don't move at all!" Jerry, despite the fuzziness he felt in his head, stopped wriggling his body, sensing the seriousness in the soldier's voice.

Jerry turned to Linda and said in a weak voice, "He's a British soldier, isn't he?"

"Yes," Linda replied as calmly as her fear would allow, "he is. Just stay still for a bit longer, Jerry."

A minute more, and with another shout of victory, the soldier gently lifted the mine out of the hole he had dug in the sand, and placed it next to his protective shield. "Right," he said to the other soldier, who had been looking on from a safer distance. "You help the girl and I'll take the lad."

The soldier helped Linda to her feet. "Come on," he said. "Let's get you both off here," and holding her gently by the arm he led her through the path of markers they had left in the sand.

The first solder, leaving his metal probe on the beach, gently picked Jerry up in his arms and said, "You've had some journey, my lad! Come on, we're almost home."

Jerry looked up weakly into the smiling face of his rescuer and asked, "Are we really on the Isle of Wight?"

"Yes, indeed you are, and very fortunate indeed to still be alive, having walked over a mined beach!"

As they were both being helped off the beach, an army medic arrived on a motorcycle and immediately took a look at Jerry's wounded head. "You've had a nasty knock there, son," he said. Jerry winced as the medic cleaned and dressed the wound. "How did it happen?"

Jerry opened his eyes and answered rather weakly, "Part of our boat hit me on the head last night as we were trying to land on the beach." He paused for a moment, looking up at Linda, and said, "Linda pulled me up out of the surf and saved my life."

The eyes of the small company of soldiers fixed on the girl standing wet and bedraggled, and the man with the peaked cap said, "I think you had better tell us where you are from and what this is all about, young lady."

CHAPTER 30

In Hospital

"This is truly unbelievable," remarked Captain James Cruickshank. He looked at Linda, who was now washed and dried and wearing a mismatch of hastily cobbled-together clothes. "Are you honestly telling me that you and your friend managed to get off Jersey and navigate right up the English Channel in a little boat with no real knowledge of where you were or where you might end up?"

"Basically, that's correct, sir," replied Linda simply.

"I'll have to confirm this with your friend, Jerry," the captain replied, still with a note of scepticism in his voice. "We'll go down to the hospital in Shanklin a little later to see how Jerry is and then he can confirm your story. And are you really sure about this story of Hitler coming to Jersey?"

"Absolutely," Linda replied, with conviction in her voice. "That's why we came here! We also have some details of where the Germans are planning on building their fortifications and placing their guns." Just then there was a loud knock on the officer's door.

"Enter," called the captain. The door opened and a young private entered and smartly saluted his commander.

"Sir," he said curtly, "we have found what appears to be the wreckage of a small boat on the beach under the cliffs, about a quarter of a mile from where the two children were found." The young soldier stopped and then added, "We also found an outboard motor and the remains of a can of diesel." Then he lifted a small wet black book up and placed it on Captain Cruickshank's table, "And we found this on the beach, sir."

"Uncle Fred's Bible!" Linda exclaimed in surprise.

"Thank you," said the captain to the private, and then turned to Linda. "So, it seems that your incredible story may well be true after all."

It was about two hours later, and Linda was waiting outside the hospital ward in the Isle of Wight town of Shanklin.

"You may come in now," said the nurse in charge of the ward, "but your friend has lost quite a bit of blood and is still quite weak, so do not overtire him."

"Okay," answered Linda with a smile. "I'll try not to be long."

Jerry looked up from his pillow as Linda approached his bed. The top of his head was swathed in a large white bandage and his right arm held across his chest in a white sling.

"Hello," he said brightly, as Linda pulled up a chair next to his bed. "How are you?"

Linda laughed. "How am I?" she retorted. "How am I? Take a look at yourself! How are you?"

"I'm well," answered Jerry, with a smile, "but I have felt better, I have to admit."

"You've looked better too," answered Linda, with a little giggle. "So," she continued, "you need to get better quickly, as the captain who helped rescue us has arranged for us to travel by train to London tomorrow. He says the information we have will be of interest to the military in London."

"Wow, I wonder who we'll be seeing!" Jerry exclaimed.

"I don't know, but I have been told that a soldier is going to go with us all the way," Linda said, with a twinkle in her eye, "so I guess that they think what we have to tell them is quite important."

"Yes, I suppose you're right," Jerry answered, with a thoughtful expression on his face as he gazed out of the window. "Just think, Linda, how important the Channel Islands will become if Hitler is assassinated whilst visiting them. Some of the people back home thought we had been forgotten about by Britain because the Islands were left undefended last year."

"Well," Linda responded, "before we can see whoever we have to see, you must be well enough to be able to travel."

"Oh, I'll be okay," Jerry replied confidently, as he sought with one hand to pull himself up a little higher on the stack of pillows that were placed behind his head. He then added as he winced with pain, "Well, at least I think I will be." Both of them laughed, relieved to be warm and safe and almost on their way to accomplish the final part of their mission.

"Look," said Linda taking out the still damp Bible and passing it to Jerry, "the soldiers found this on the beach when they were checking our story."

Jerry smiled. "I'm so glad they found it, I was wishing we'd looked for it this morning. I have been thinking about Uncle Fred again and how he said he had been saved twice; once by God from his bad ways and again when his ship was torpedoed. You know God has saved us more than twice."

"How come?" Linda quizzed.

Well, firstly from that motorbike before we had left Jersey, then when they started to shoot at us from St. Martin, and if those Germans who caught Uncle Fred had seen him throwing those diesel cans off the cliffs one of them should have at least shined a torch down towards where we were at the bottom of the cliffs. Then there was last night when we ran headlong into the rocks in the boat; really, we could both so easily have drowned. Then walking all that way over a mined beach without being blown up. Do you remember that promise from the Bible that Uncle Fred read to us about passing through the waters?"

"Yes, I remember," said Linda thoughtfully.

"Well, did it not also say that when we walk through the fire we would not be burned? Well, God kept us through the waters and again this morning on the beach as we walked through the fire of that minefield. You know, Linda, the more I think about it the more I realise that God must be a real God Whom I can safely trust."

Just then the nurse came, "Okay, young lady, I think you two have had quite long enough together. Time for Jerry to take a nap."

"Okay," said Linda. "I am not sure where I'll be tonight, but I'll be in tomorrow, hopefully to take you out."

"You may or may not take him out," scolded the nurse. "It depends on how well he progresses." Pausing, she pulled out some damp and battered papers from a file she was carrying, and showing them to the two friends, she said, "I am not sure but I guess that these papers you had on you when you arrived might just be important!"

"Wow!" said Jerry, "They certainly are. How stupid of us to have forgotten about them. They show where the German Headquarters are stationed on Jersey. We can't afford to lose those."

"Ah," said the nurse in a teasing manner, "so you do come from Jersey." Then stopping and sighing, she added, "I went there about four years ago. What a beautiful Island it is! We had a wonderful time there; we went swimming in the sea at St. Brelade's Bay and at Grève de Lecq."

"Did you like our Martello Towers around the Island?" asked Linda.

"Martello Towers?" questioned the nurse, wearing a puzzled expression. "What are they?"

"Martello Towers are those lovely granite towers which can be seen dotted around the Island. They were built over a hundred years ago to defend the Island from the French," Linda explained excitedly.

"Oh, those," the nurse answered, the light suddenly dawning on her face. "Yes, they were very interesting and beautiful too. Pity they didn't keep the Germans away as well as the French!"

"Too true," interjected Jerry, with strong passion in his voice. "My dad says that if we had tried to defend the Island there would have been a bigger bloodbath than there was when we were bombed and machine-gunned just before the Germans invaded."

"Were you bombed?" the nurse asked in a surprised manner.

"Oh, yes," replied Linda.

"Yes, we certainly were! I remember the earth shook and I just blindly ran, not knowing where I was going!" said Jerry. "I found myself crouched next to a wall trembling, expecting everyone around me to have been killed. I found out later that nine were dead including a good friend of my dad's, who was driving a tomato lorry down by the harbour. Guernsey was bombed too, they came off worse than Jersey, with about thirty-five dead. The Germans said afterwards that had they known the Islands were undefended they wouldn't have bombed us. I didn't believe them!"

"Oh," the nurse replied, slightly taken aback. "I didn't realise it had been as bad as that in Jersey. It's been pretty horrendous on mainland England too, but with the occupation it seems you've had it worse," she said with tears in her eyes.

Jerry and Linda smiled bravely at each other. It had been hard, but it had brought quite an adventure for them!

"Okay," said the nurse, smiling softly, "you've had long enough to visit this 'old soldier' for today. If he rests and makes some good progress then maybe, just maybe, he will be fit enough to leave tomorrow. It will depend on what the doctor says."

Linda picked up the plans and papers handed to her by the nurse, and said to Jerry, "Maybe I had better look after these tonight?"

"Too right," answered Jerry with a smile. "This hospital bed is uncomfortable enough without having to share it with those plans!"

CHAPTER 31

On Their Way

Jerry woke early the next morning. The July sun flooded in through the partially opened blinds that covered the two large windows of the hospital ward. He felt much better after a good night's sleep, but still had a slight headache and a continual ache in his arm. However, he was sure today was the day that he and Linda would be allowed to get away to London. It was vital that they pass on to the authorities the information they had brought from Jersey. He felt that today was a real day of destiny, not just for Linda and him, but also for the whole world.

Linda arrived at Jerry's side with an army sergeant, at the same time as the doctor. "Will you let him out today?" she pleaded with the doctor, as he stood reading some notes at the bottom of Jerry's bed.

The doctor looked over the top of his spectacles at Jerry. "Well, how are you feeling today?" he enquired.

"Oh, much better than yesterday, thank you," Jerry answered enthusiastically.

"I'd like you to get up and try and walk to the end of the ward for me," the doctor said, his eyes narrowing as he felt for Jerry's pulse. Jerry carefully pulled back the sheets and rather clumsily dragged his legs over the side of the bed. Linda helped him to his feet and he stood for a moment swaying unsteadily as a wave of dizziness came over him.

"That's alright," the doctor said encouragingly. "You may feel a bit dizzy for a while. Just take your time, and when you're ready try to walk to the end of the ward and back." Jerry stood holding on to the nurse before attempting to walk up the ward. The nurse walked alongside of him and together they made it to the end of the ward and back again. Jerry, on returning to his bed, was feeling much brighter and a lot more confident.

"Well," the doctor said thoughtfully, "I should like to have kept you in here for another day, but I have been asked by a very senior army officer to release you and let you travel to London." The doctor paused as he again took up Jerry's notes from the end of the bed. He looked them over before adding, "This sergeant and a medic will accompany you. That being the case, you are free to go, young man, but..." he continued, pausing to gain Jerry's full attention, "you must be careful and not overdo it. You still have a nasty gash on that head of yours and you may experience bouts of sickness and dizziness. If you do, you must lie down and rest."

"Okay," said Jerry meekly. "I will be careful and try and do exactly what you say."

It took Jerry quite a while to get ready to leave the hospital. His arm was painful to touch and made every movement difficult and awkward. Each time he stood up, waves of dizziness and sickness washed over him, but he was determined he was not going to allow this to stop him making the trip to London. At last, with the help of the nurse, he was ready. They set off down the ward.

Once outside, the army sergeant led them to a small canvas-topped Land Rover parked on a grassed area opposite the main entrance to the hospital. A man in army uniform, wearing a large white armband with a red cross, was waiting in the driver's seat.

"This is Brian, and my name is Cuthbert," said the sergeant.

Jerry and Linda glanced at each other and made an unsuccessful attempt to suppress a fit of giggles.

"Sorry!" Linda said, only just managing to control her laughter, and blushing a little. "The fact is," Linda explained, "we have never met anyone called Cuthbert before."

The big burly sergeant laughed too, "Neither have I,"

he said. "It was my grandmother's fault. When I was born, my parents couldn't decide what to call me, and when my grandmother came to see me, she said that I looked like a Cuthbert and so that's what they called me!"

Jerry, managing to smother his giggles, looked up at Cuthbert and smiled politely, thinking, *I'm glad I didn't have your grandmother!* The children clambered into the back of the Land Rover and Cuthbert climbed into the front passenger seat. Brian quickly started the engine, put it into gear and shot out of the hospital car park on to the main Shanklin road as if they had no time to lose.

It took about three quarters of an hour to travel across the island from Shanklin to Yarmouth in the rickety old army vehicle. Brian, although a medic, seemed oblivious to Jerry's condition, as he swung the little Land Rover around bends, and sped up and down hills at what Linda thought was a breakneck speed. Jerry, who was sitting in the back next to Linda, was by now feeling most uncomfortable, as he tried to support his aching arm and at the same time suppress the ever-growing feeling of sickness and dizziness that washed over him. Eventually, he could suppress it no longer, and when his stomach gave a big heave, he put his head out of the open side of the vehicle and let it all out!

"Hey, Brian," Cuthbert said. "Better slow down. Don't forget the kid's been through a lot in the last few days!"

"Okay, Sergeant," Brian said breezily, slowing the Land Rover to a more comfortable pace.

Once at the pretty little town of Yarmouth, they boarded a small ferry that would take them across to Lymington on the south coast of England. The ferry was tightly packed with all kinds of different people, including ordinary civilians and army personnel. To Jerry, the ferry was pure bliss after the car ride he had just experienced. He felt more comfortable on this boat than he had in the Land Rover and he wasted no time in letting the two soldiers know.

"So," enquired Brian for the first time, "how is this head of yours and exactly how did you manage to make such a mess of yourself, young man?"

"It's really a very long story," Jerry replied, "and if you don't mind I'll tell it all to you on another occasion, as right now I'm still feeling very sick from your terrible driving and my head is spinning like a top."

They all laughed at Jerry's comments about the driving before settling down in silence to enjoy the trip to the mainland.

The ferry crossing was relatively short and trouble-free. Cuthbert, with his army status, was able to get both children through the various checkpoints without too much difficulty. When arriving in the little harbour of Lymington, they disembarked, and Cuthbert and Brian escorted them to a large black car parked alongside the pier and opened the door for them to get in.

Another sergeant with stripes on his arm was the driver. He greeted the other two soldiers, and then looking at Jerry and Linda said, "So these are our two young heroes from Jersey."

Cuthbert looked at him and smiled as he climbed into the front passenger seat. "Yes, they are and they have a very important meeting in London this afternoon," he responded, "so let's get to Southampton double-quick!"

"Not too quick!" interjected Jerry sharply. "Remember, I am still recovering from Brian's driving!" They all laughed heartily and the driver started the car and pulled away gently.

"The plan is," said Cuthbert over his shoulder, "to catch the London train from Southampton and meet up with someone who Captain Cruickshank has made contact with." Then he added with a wry smile, "By the way, he gave me my orders, after speaking to London, that I wasn't to let you two out of my sight until we get there, so I guess you have some important information!"

Linda narrowed her eyes and said, "Yes, we have, but it will stay with us until we meet whoever your captain has been in contact with."

The car pulled into the station at Southampton and the driver called a cheery "Goodbye" and "Good Luck," as the four of them clambered out of the car, Jerry still feeling rather dizzy and a bit awkward. They waved goodbye to the driver as he sped off in the opposite direction.

Brian, looking at his watch, said, "Quick, we have just got time to catch the 12:15 train to Waterloo." The four broke into a trot and hurried through the station doors and along a causeway filled with people. Linda thought that she had never seen so large a crowd all in one place. Jerry struggled to keep up with the others, and at the same time protect his arm, as he pushed his way through the people. Brian kept close to him, and helped him along as much as he could.

On arriving on the platform Jerry and Linda both stopped dead in their tracks as they gazed in awe at the train standing at the platform. Cuthbert stopped too and turned to them in astonishment. "What's the matter?" he asked. "Don't tell me you have never seen a train before?"

"No," sighed Jerry dreamily. "Well, at least not one this size, it's huge! Our little railway along the seafront in Jersey stopped running about five years ago after a fire at St. Aubin's Station."

"Well, come on. We can't stand here gawking all day," Brian said jovially. "We had better take you for a ride on a real train! Come on, I'll help you up."

Jerry and Linda, having bagged window seats, looked out excitedly as the train pulled away from the station and began to pick up speed. Little wisps of steam from the engine funnel passed the window and disappeared rapidly. The dense woods and bright green fields were so different to Jersey, where the fields were either a muddy brown or filled with the leaves of the potato crop.

Jerry sat transfixed at the flashing scenery as it whizzed by. "I'm sure that I have never travelled so fast in my life," he said in amazement. The train thundered towards London with its 'clickerty-clack, clickerty-clack' on the rails. Both youngsters kept their noses pressed excitedly to the window.

"Wow," said Jerry in astonishment, "look at those cows, Linda, they are black and white! Not a bit like our brown Jersey cows!"

"I've an uncle who lives in Worcester, he has cows like that, but he always likes us to send him some of our butter because it's a lot richer and creamier than the butter he can make," explained Linda.

Brian, who had been listening to the two children, told them, "They're called Friesians! Right enough though, young lassie, the milk isn't quite as good as what you would get from your Jersey cows."

All too soon grey and red buildings came into view, and the train began slowing down as it entered the outskirts of a large town.

CHAPTER 32

London

"This is Basingstoke," Cuthbert informed the two enthusiastic young people whom he was beginning to like and admire the more time he spent in their company. He sat in the small compartment of the carriage looking earnestly at their excited faces and wondered what had made them embark on such a perilous journey over one hundred miles of water, with no certainty of ever reaching their destination.

"How much further to London?" Linda asked

"Oh, I reckon another hour or so, miss," Cuthbert replied.

"That is provided there is no air raid on when we get there," Brian added. "Last September you could hardly get into London at all, because of what we called 'The Blitz'. Buildings were on fire, bombs were falling, people dying everywhere. It was terrible, really awful, but our fighter pilots did a sterling job. How they did it, I will never know, but they stopped the Luftwaffe in their tracks. We still have air raids, of course, but nothing like those we had last year."

"We had an air raid in Jersey," Linda chipped in. "Jerry was there in the town when it happened. Weren't you, Jerry?"

"Yes," Jerry answered. "It happened two days before the invasion when these Heinkel bombers suddenly appeared out of nowhere, dropped bombs and fired their machine guns all over the harbour area of the town and round the coast at La Rocque harbour. I was lucky, I dived for cover near an old stonewall, and was okay, but nine people were killed."

"My dad said that the Germans were sorry afterwards. It

seems they did not know that Jersey had no defences, or they would not have bombed us," Linda added.

"Well, I don't think they were one bit sorry for all the death and destruction they caused in London last year," Cuthbert retorted.

The train had stopped at a station, but was now on its way again, gathering up speed as it puffed its way towards London. The two continued to look out of the window excitedly as the train sped on towards its final destination.

"How's your head and arm doing, Jerry?" Brian enquired kindly.

"Not too bad, just both still a bit sore," Jerry replied.

"And your stomach after Brian's driving?" Cuthbert added.

"No comment," Jerry responded with a wry smile.

Linda felt the pockets of her mismatched clothes, to check that she still had the various plans. Having assured herself that they were safe and sound she felt a larger bulkier thing in her right pocket, and after a moment of fidgeting with it she pulled it out and exclaimed, "Look, Jerry, I still have this."

"Mercy me," Brian remarked. "Where did that Bible come from?"

"My uncle," replied Jerry. "He started out with us, but was caught by the Germans in Guernsey."

"He was caught in Guernsey? But I thought you had come from Jersey?" Cuthbert questioned.

"We did, but we had to get more diesel in Guernsey," Jerry replied.

Jerry explained how his uncle had known people in Guernsey and had managed to get diesel from them and thrown it down off the cliffs. He told Brian and Cuthbert how they had heard the Germans shouting and a shot fired, and then Uncle Fred calling out to tell them to get away.

"That's just amazing," responded the sergeant.

"So is your uncle a Christian?" asked Brian with interest.

"Yes, he is," Jerry responded. "He told us he was a wild

man, but then heard someone preaching in Belfast and became a Christian."

"And after that," Linda added with enthusiasm, "he was invited to someone's house and ended up missing his boat, which was torpedoed during the last war and everyone on it died."

"Wow! That is some story," Cuthbert remarked. "It makes you wonder if there really is a God after all."

"Oh, my grandmother believes there is," Brian declared. "She made me go to Sunday school every Sunday. I can still recite verses from the Bible that I learnt there."

"Go on, then," said Cuthbert with a smile. "Give us some."

"Well, I know all the 'I am's' in John's gospel," Brian said. "If we could say them all, we were given a small leather Bible quite like the one Linda is holding. They all started with 'Jesus said'," he explained. "Jesus said, 'I am the Good Shepherd: the Good Shepherd giveth His life for the sheep,' John chapter ten verse eleven; Jesus said, 'I am the Light of the world: he that followeth Me shall not walk in darkness, but shall have the light of life,' John chapter eight verse twelve; Jesus said, 'I am the door: by Me if any man enter in, he shall be saved,' John chapter ten verse nine; Jesus said, 'I am the way, the truth, and the life: no man cometh unto the Father, but by Me,' John chapter fourteen verse six…"

"Hey, that's the verse from the Bible which Uncle Fred had underlined," both children said in unison as Brian quoted the last one.

"That page had a bookmark in it and the verse was underlined," Linda exclaimed in amazement that Brian had quoted the exact same verse.

"I remember, we read it when we were wondering about what had happened to Uncle Fred," Jerry added. "We were trying to work out what it meant."

"Well, in the Sunday school we were told that the Lord Jesus was saying that He was the only way to heaven," Brian explained.

"Do you think it means He is the only way to heaven?" Linda asked intently.

"Well," Brian said thoughtfully, "I learnt another verse as well from John's gospel that went...oh here, pass me that Bible and I'll try and find it."

Linda passed the small black Bible to Brian, who commenced to thumb through its still damp pages until he found what he was looking for. "Here it is," he said. "This is underlined as well: 'For God so loved the world, that He gave His only begotten Son, that whosoever believeth in Him should not perish, but have everlasting life,' John chapter three verse sixteen."

"What does 'begotten' mean?" enquired Linda.

"Well, I'm not very sure," Brian confessed, "but if I remember right, I think I was told it meant 'God's unique Son'."

"You mean that there is no-one else like Him?" Jerry asked.

"There's no one like my colonel," commented Cuthbert, who had been listening attentively to the conversation. "He's a one-off, is old Colonel Sommerville!"

"I can see that there has never been anyone like the Lord Jesus," Linda chipped in, ignoring the sergeant's comments. "I mean, He had to be special to do all those miracles and things."

"Well, I was taught that He was the only way to heaven and that if I wanted to go there I needed to trust Him as my Saviour and be really sorry for my sins. My Sunday school teacher used to say that it was because of my sins that the Lord Jesus died on the cross."

"That's just what my uncle believes too!" Jerry responded with enthusiasm, before asking, "Have you trusted Him, Brian?"

Brian was a little taken aback by such a forthright question and stammered over his answer. "Well, err, no, I mean I, well it's sort of...oh, I guess I just have not thought about it since my Sunday school days."

"London!" called Cuthbert excitedly, as the train began to slow, glad to get an opportunity to change the subject.

They saw some large, dark, impressive-looking Victorian-style houses out of the window. Jerry excitedly said, "Hey, we have houses a bit like some of those on Jersey."

Linda looked across and said, "And they have them in Guernsey too."

Eventually the train slowed almost to a walking pace and the rapidity of the sound of the wheels on the rails changed to a more unusual noise as the train trundled over the various points systems as it neared its terminus at Waterloo Station.

"Hey," Linda shouted out suddenly, "we're on a bridge, crossing over water."

"That," answered the sergeant with some amusement, "is the River Thames and if you look up there," he said, pointing, "you can see Big Ben."

"Sorry to correct you, Sergeant," Brian butted in, "but that is not quite true. You cannot actually see Big Ben! Big Ben is the main bell in the Tower but the actual clock that you can see is called 'The Great Westminster Clock'."

"Hey, I never knew that," said Linda.

"Swot," Cuthbert answered with a wry smile on his face as he looked across at Brian and then down at the two children. "Perhaps," he added, with a touch of sarcasm in his voice, "Brian, here, will be able to give you a tour of this once fine city. That is, of course, after your business here is completed."

The train came to a halt with a gentle bump. Brian opened the door of the compartment that led into the corridor. Cuthbert led the way down the corridor to the door, and after opening it he jumped down the short step onto the platform. He held out his hand to the children and carefully helped them down from the train. "Welcome to Waterloo Station," he said.

Jerry looked up and seeing what appeared to be a shattered roof, exclaimed, "Wow, what caused that?"

"German bombers, last October," Brian commented sombrely.

"They certainly made a mess, didn't they?" Linda remarked, looking above her head.

"Not just the roof," Brian answered. "They wrecked much of the station and it's still only working on a very small capacity." He paused as they surveyed the mass of broken glass and twisted metal above them.

As they walked down the platform towards the exit, a tall middle-aged man dressed in a faded green uniform, and with a gaunt-looking face and distinctly projecting jaw came towards them and introduced himself.

"Good afternoon," he said with a smile, as he acknowledged both Cuthbert's and Brian's salute. "My name is Colonel Fleming from the Department of Strategic Planning. I presume these are our two young refugees from Jersey?" he said, his face breaking into a broad smile.

"Yes, sir," answered Cuthbert in clipped tones, standing bolt upright in the 'attention' position.

"At ease, both of you," the colonel said to the two soldiers. Then turning to the children, he said, "I have come to take you immediately to a debriefing session in Whitehall, because if what you have told Captain Cruickshank on the Isle of Wight is true, we haven't got a moment to lose." Then turning smartly on his heels, he said to all four of them, "Follow me."

"What's a debriefing session?" Linda asked the two soldiers curiously.

"Oh, it's where they ask you lots of questions and you give them as much information as possible," the sergeant answered helpfully. "It's really nothing to worry about at all."

Outside the station, another large black car was waiting for them, and the colonel opened the rear door to allow them all in. In the back of the car were two bench seats. The first bench seat tipped forward allowing access into the one behind it. Jerry, Linda and Brian scrambled in and sat down whilst Colonel Fleming and Cuthbert climbed into the seats in front. The colonel gave an order to the driver and the car moved off.

Jerry and Linda turned in their seats to look out of the rear window.

"Have you ever been to London before?" asked the colonel in a conversational manner.

"No, never," Linda replied, without turning her eyes away from the window. Jerry and Linda stared goggle-eyed as they passed tall elegant-looking buildings and occasionally observed a gap where a building had once stood. On another road, they passed the derelict shell of a building, causing Linda to ask, "I presume there are so many derelict and missing buildings because of what you call 'The Blitz'?"

"Yes," answered Brian simply.

"To have seen London at its best," the colonel added, "you would have needed to have come before the war." Then turning around to face Jerry, he asked, "So how's the head, young fellow? I was told that you had damaged yourself when you were washed up on the Isle of Wight."

"Yes," Linda interjected, before Jerry had chance to respond. "Our boat was caught in the breakers and smashed onto the rocks around Freshwater Bay and we were thrown right into the sea. Poor Jerry was knocked right out when part of our boat hit his head, but thankfully he managed to get to shore," she said modestly without mentioning her part in pulling Jerry from the sea.

"Quite remarkable," the colonel answered with a look of awe on his face. "But you're doing okay now?"

"Yes, thank you," replied Jerry. "Just a dull ache in my arm and an occasional sharp pain in my head, but apart from that I'm fine."

It was not long before the car came to a standstill outside an impressive, large, white building with lots of green-coloured windows and large round pillars standing elegantly right along its front. There were white stone steps leading from the pavement to a wide entrance with glass doors.

"Here we are," said the colonel. "Now let's go in, they're waiting for you."

They all climbed out of the car and the colonel led them

up the large flight of stone steps towards the main entrance. Here there was a large and very heavy revolving door. Each had to wait their turn before jumping into their own small section as it rotated around. Jerry remembered a time as a youngster when he had been caught playing in one of these doors in one of Jersey's large shops. He winced as he recalled the telling off he had received from his dad.

Once inside the doors they found themselves in a large cavernous foyer. It had a polished staircase running up both sides, and the ceiling was so high that Linda, gazing upwards at it, exclaimed, "How do they ever paint up there?" Cuthbert and Brian both smiled to themselves, but the colonel showed no real interest in the comment.

The colonel turned to the two soldiers who had accompanied the children from the Isle of Wight. "You two may go through into the canteen and get yourselves something to eat, whilst I take these two young friends upstairs."

"Thank you, sir," responded Cuthbert enthusiastically. "We could do with something to eat."

"You're telling me," Brian replied, licking his lips.

Jerry and Linda glanced at each other rather anxiously, wondering whether they were going to get anything to eat. The colonel, observing their concerned faces, turned to them with a twinkle in his eye and said, "Don't you worry. You will be eating too, but not in the canteen. You will be dining with the senior military in the Officer's Mess."

"I might have known it," Cuthbert replied with a laugh. "You two eating with the top brass, and us with military rations in the canteen. Well, if it's really good save us a bit, please!"

Both Jerry and Linda laughed at the comical faces of the two soldiers. "We will," they answered.

Jerry and Linda were then escorted up the staircase which, had Jerry felt better and had he not been walking behind what seemed to be a very important man, he'd have liked to have done two at a time. After walking down a very long corridor, the colonel stopped in front of a large green door and knocked sharply on it. A voice from behind the door called crisply, "Enter." The colonel turned the brass doorknob, pushed open the door and led the way into the room. Jerry and Linda found themselves in a large airy room with three enormous windows on one side and a high vaulted ceiling. There was a large wooden table taking centre position, on which lay what looked like maps of Jersey. To the side was a smaller table which was laid up with a spread of food unlike anything Jerry and Linda had ever seen before.

"Good afternoon. So you must be Jerry and Linda?" Jerry looked up to see a tall man with a balding head and a grey moustache. He looked very much like one of the caricature sergeant majors that the children had seen in some of the newspaper cartoons.

The children, rather awestruck at their surroundings and conscious of the vital importance of their mission, gazed up at the major and replied, "Good afternoon, sir."

CHAPTER 33

Telling What They Knew

Jerry and Linda found themselves seated at the large table in front of the tall man with the moustache. "I am Major Simmonds of the Army Intelligence Corps," he said, while moving one of the plans across the table. "Colonel Fleming you have already met, and this is Wing Commander Talbert from the RAF." He introduced a much younger man, who said hello to the children in a friendly manner that made both of them feel more at ease.

"My, look at those bandages," the Wing Commander commented. "Why, you have been in the wars, haven't you?" he said, looking at Jerry.

"This happened to this young man on his arrival on the Isle of Wight," Colonel Fleming answered. "Remarkable really; these two young people escape from an occupied island and risk everything to see us with some vital information, and sail a tiny boat right up the English Channel, and then Jerry gets injured just when he's almost home and dry."

"I certainly wasn't dry when I was thrown out of the boat," Jerry added, smiling.

"I can imagine you were not at all," commented Major Simmonds before continuing, "And this," he said introducing the last person in the room, "is Mr Davies from the Government. His brief is to report back to the Prime Minister's office on anything that you may tell us that will be of interest to those in the highest authority." He paused as he looked at the two tired children in front of them and, as if changing his plans, said, "But I think we will eat first and talk later as

I am sure you must be very hungry after your trip up from Southampton."

"That would be lovely," replied Linda quickly in case the major changed his mind. "We are both rather hungry."

"Well then, go and get yourself a plate and help yourself from the table in the corner, and I will order the tea and coffee, or would you children just prefer milk?"

"No, tea will be lovely," replied Linda for them both, wanting to seem as grown up as possible.

He lifted the receiver on the telephone and ordered the tea and coffee to be brought to them.

The two children lifted a plate each from the table and looked with excitement at the trays of food on offer. There were things here that the children had not seen for ages back on their little Island. Sandwiches made with real bread and filled with ham or cheese, cold sausages, apples and pears and even a few small sweet biscuits. "This is amazing," Linda said, as she helped herself to a sausage. "We have not had food like this back home for quite a while."

"You can say that again," added Jerry with a smile, as he placed another sandwich on his already overflowing plate.

"Um, er, well," mumbled the bemused major with a rather embarrassed laugh, "we do tend to do rather well for food, working in here!"

The children soon cleared their plates as well as most of what was on the table, and sat sipping their tea from the white china teacups.

"Well then," said the major, anxious to find out what the children had to tell them. "I understand you two have come all the way from Jersey with some very interesting news."

Linda hesitated before putting her hand inside her coat and pulling out the plans given to Jerry by the Bailiff before leaving Jersey. "Well, we think it's terribly important," she announced to all in the room. "That's why we tried to escape from Jersey in order to come and tell you!"

The major's face changed as he answered, "Quite! So, now start from the beginning and tell us why and how you were able to get away from Jersey without being caught, and how you came to arrive in the Isle of Wight, and everything you know."

Jerry began to relate all he knew about the rumours of Hitler's proposed visit to Jersey and about the extra troops that were apparently being drafted in for that event. He told the major how Linda's parents had been caught by the Germans, and how they had had to change their plans as a result. He showed him on the map of Jersey the exact place where he, Linda and Uncle Fred had launched the boat and how they had managed to escape from Jersey. He gave a detailed account of the dreadful events that had taken place on the cliffs of Guernsey and told the major about his fears for the safety of his uncle. Every now and then Linda interrupted, adding information she thought Jerry had either forgotten or overlooked. The two of them compared their plans with those on the table, pointing out to the men where they knew there were German troops billeted on the Island, as well as where they thought they were constructing gun and lookout positions.

After what seemed like a long time, Jerry and Linda looked at each other, then Jerry added with a feeling of satisfaction, "Well, I think we have told you just about everything we know. We thought, as many in Jersey do, that if Hitler does visit the Island the only way for him to get there is either by sea or air, so that would be the best time to attack him! We can't let him succeed in getting on to the Island because that would be too late, as once on the Island he would be too heavily defended, and our mission would have failed."

There was a prolonged silence from all in the room. The four men looked from one to the other and then at the two children who sat with baited breath, waiting to hear whether these men would be able to put some sort of plan into action.

It was Wing Commander Talbert, who broke the silence, "Well, what you two have told us agrees one hundred percent with what our intelligence has been reporting to us for the past fortnight. That is, that an important German leader was planning to visit the Channel Islands sometime very soon. Even though our intelligence suggested it was going to be Hitler himself, we had not ruled out the possibility that it might have been Goebbels, his propaganda minister." The Wing Commander paused and coughed uneasily. He was clearly trying to find the right words to express what he wanted to say. He cleared his throat again before adding, "The Prime Minister considered this piece of intelligence of such importance that two whole squadrons were on standby ready to intercept any boat or plane travelling to the Island that we believed had such an important person on board." He paused again and rubbed his chin with his right hand whilst fingering uneasily the plans lying on the table. "Unfortunately," he added, his voice uneasy with emotion, "the latest intelligence suggests that the planned visit was cancelled forty-eight hours ago and will now not take place." A crushing stillness filled the room as both Jerry and Linda gazed in stunned silence at each other and then at the four men as this piece of information penetrated their minds.

Linda spoke up first, "You mean that Hitler will not be visiting Jersey after all?"

"It would seem not," the major answered. "Well, at least not according to our intelligence."

"Your intelligence may be wrong," Jerry suggested in desperation.

"Possibly," the Wing Commander answered calmly, "but our intelligence comes from several very reliable sources. We believe that Adolf Hitler has, in fact, gone to his mountain retreat, the Berghoff, and plans to be there for the next fortnight at least." He paused, looking sympathetically at the two youngsters as they sat dejectedly before him. "I'm so very sorry," he continued. "After all that you two have done risking your lives in order to bring us this information, I know how you must feel." He stopped and a silence filled the room as the four adults felt keenly the disappointment that they saw etched on the children's faces.

After a long pause Mr Davies, the Government Minister,

spoke, "I must say though, I am certain the Prime Minister will be most interested in the information you have furnished us with, particularly as to the whereabouts of the German garrisons on the Island, as well as where you believe they are planning to install gun emplacements and fortifications. Mr Churchill will be most interested in these things as he has a great affection for what I have heard him refer to as 'our dear Channel Islands', and I know he is very concerned to know how the Islanders are coping under German occupation." He got up from his seat and walked over to look out of a window, before turning and once again breaking the silence. "I hope that it is of some comfort to you to know that your effort has not been in vain. These plans will be studied in great detail and be a huge help in planning any strategy to retake the Channel Islands for Britain in the future, and on behalf of the Government I would like to thank you two youngsters profusely for the sacrifices you have made in leaving family, friends and home." He stopped as he walked back to the table and again studied the plans that both Jerry and Linda had unfolded on the table.

The two youngsters found it hard to contain their bitter disappointment. They thought about all the dreams that they had shared with each other of how their information was going to be the means of the German leader being assassinated, and as a result bringing a swift end to the war. Now these same dreams had been turned to dust. They tried hard to fight back their tears, but Linda found herself unable to stifle her sobs as she thought of her parents, the farm, her Island and Jerry's Uncle Fred. In her mind she could still hear Jerry's uncle shouting from the cliff, "Get away." What about the shots she had heard fired? What had become of Uncle Fred? Was he a prisoner? Was he dead? Then her mind flashed to the journey they had made and how she had dragged Jerry up the beach when they had been washed up on the Isle of Wight. The wing commander walked round and put his hand on her shoulder as he tried to comfort her. Jerry felt helpless as he struggled with his own broken and crushed spirit.

Colonel Fleming kind-heartedly spoke to the children, "Each one of us in this room appreciates so much what you two have done and the risks you took to get this vital information here to us. You said goodbye to your family and escaped from Jersey and, dicing with death, sailed all the way up the English Channel. You were both very brave indeed! Believe me when I say we think you deserve a medal for what you have done. We are proud of you, we really are." He rose from his green leather chair and held out his hand to shake both Jerry's and Linda's and added, "If Hitler had ventured out of his safety zone, believe me we'd have done all we could to have got him. As it is, he has decided not to take that risk, which means this war is just going to last a little longer. We have somewhere for you two to stay tonight in London, and then we will arrange to get you both out of the city and into the country where you will be safe for the remainder of the war."

"What?" gasped Linda in disbelief. "Jerry and me sit out the rest of the war here? No way! We are going back to Jersey straight away, aren't we, Jerry?"

"Yes," replied Jerry determinedly, "we want to go back to our families and our Island."

"I am afraid that is not possible," replied Mr Davies. "I am sorry to say that there is no way to repatriate you both during wartime. We may, however, through our contacts be able to inform your parents about your welfare, which I am sure will be a big relief to them."

As he ended his sentence, Jerry spoke up again. "No, sir, that's not good enough! We want to go home, back to Jersey. We managed to get here and we will manage to get home too! My brother died as a baby and so my parents didn't want to lose me as well. No, Linda and I will be going back to Jersey."

CHAPTER 34

Dreams Of Home

Darkness was falling as Colonel Fleming led the two children out of the imposing building, down the white stone steps and onto the wide street in front.

"Excuse me, sir," said a familiar voice from the top of the steps. All three looked round to see Cuthbert and Brian standing smiling at them, "If we may, sir, well, what I am trying to say, sir," explained the sergeant a little sheepishly, "is, as we have been entrusted with these two from the Isle of Wight, would we be allowed to accompany them to their new destination?"

"Well," the colonel stammered, caught a little off guard. "Well," he said again, "I was just going to hail a taxi and travel with them to the Hunters Inn at Kilburn until we can arrange for more permanent accommodation for them."

"We can do that, sir," offered Brian, still carrying his medical bag slung loosely over his shoulder.

The colonel paused and considered the offer, and then looking at the children suggested, "I'm sure you would both rather travel with these two handsome young soldiers than an old fuddy-duddy like me, wouldn't you?"

"Oh, yes," Linda replied, before catching herself and blushing with embarrassment, "but I didn't mean you were an old fuddy-duddy!" All five standing on the pavement laughed and the colonel informed them that he would arrange for someone to escort them both the next day to a safer environment away from London and the air raids. He shook both their hands again and wished them both farewell and Godspeed, and then marched briskly up the steps. As he got to the top he turned and gave them a salute, before passing through the revolving doors and back into the building.

Well young'uns," asked Brian, as his colleague attempted to hail a taxi. "How'd it go?" He could see from the sullen expressions on their faces that they were unhappy.

"They already knew just about all our news," Linda replied dejectedly. "Their intelligence knew about Hitler planning to visit Jersey even before we did."

"So that was what it was all about," exclaimed Brian, as a black taxi pulled up alongside to pick them up. "The sergeant and I had been trying to work out why you had come. We knew it must be very important news when you were invited to meet the bigwigs here in London."

"Um," said Jerry, with a scornful frown on his face as he clambered into the back of the taxi. "If we had known that they already knew about our news we would never have left our home and family, and now they won't let us go back either!"

Both soldiers looked at each other and then back at the children. "We know your parents are still in Jersey," Cuthbert said kindly, as Brian gave their destination to the taxi driver, "but surely the authorities can find a way to get word to them to let them know you are both safe. You can then stay here in safety until the end of the war."

"No!" Jerry said, with dogged determination. "We want to go back to Jersey! We want to go back home to our parents."

"Well, I just can't see how you can," Brian replied. "At least not until after the war is over anyway."

"That's what everyone seems to say," Linda stated, "but if we could get here we are sure we can get back, as long as we can get a boat of some sort to get us across the Channel."

"But listen," said Cuthbert firmly. "You told us you were worried you'd missed the south coast of England when you came up here, and from the tip of Cornwall to Dover that coast is about four hundred miles long! How will you ever manage to find a tiny Island like Jersey that is only about four miles long?"

"It's actually a bit bigger than that," Jerry corrected him. "It's nine miles by five miles, but nearly doubles that size when the tide is out!"

"Even so," argued Cuthbert, "you'd never manage to find it, and even if you did how would you get back on shore without being caught or shot by the Germans? Remember, you were fortunate to get off the Island but you may not be so lucky getting back."

The two children lapsed into silence as the taxi trundled through the rapidly darkening streets of the city. Suddenly Linda's optimistic outlook took over again.

"Well, we will make it," she said boldly.

"Maybe it is something we should pray about," Jerry added, as he looked thoughtfully out of the window.

The taxi came to a stop outside a very old red brick building with leaded windows. The taxi driver leaned back in his seat, and sliding open the glass partition between him and his passengers, said breezily, "Here we are. Hunters Inn, Kilburn."

As the four climbed out of the taxi they heard Cuthbert exclaim in alarm and disgust to Brian, "Hey! The colonel was supposed to be bringing them but he left it to us, and now we have to pay the taxi fare as well! What a cheek." He dug in his trouser pockets for some change. "It's just typical of these high-ranking army officers!" Brian, Jerry and Linda all laughed while the sergeant grudgingly handed his money over to the taxi driver.

"Much obliged," the driver said, shutting his window and then driving off, leaving them standing in the small cobbled car park of the inn.

"Come on," said Cuthbert. "Let's get you two settled in and see if they have room for Brian and me as well."

Once inside the inn, Linda and Jerry were shown to their bedrooms, which were opposite each other down a long, narrow corridor.

"I think you'll find everything you require here," said the young maid as she opened the door to Linda's room.

Linda stepped through the door into a small room with a single bed and a dressing table. The maid pulled the top of the bedcovers down and straightened the eiderdown before adding, "The bathroom's at the end of the corridor. Now just you remember there is a war on, so no more than half a bath. Have a good night." She then crossed the passage and opened the door into Jerry's room. Then, pushing past Brian and Cuthbert, said briskly, "You two follow me, there's space in the dormitory room down here."

"We'll see you in the morning," Cuthbert called as they obediently followed the maid down the passageway.

It was much later that night that Jerry heard an incessant knocking on his bedroom door. Sleepily, he called through the darkness, "Who's there?"

"It's me, Linda," the familiar voice replied. "I need to speak to you."

Jerry climbed wearily out of bed, undid the lock and opened the door.

"Listen," Linda said, her eyes bright with excitement, "I have just realised why we left Jersey to come here."

"Why?" Jerry asked, rubbing his eyes.

"So that God could speak to us."

"Whatever do you mean?"

"Well, if we had stayed in Jersey we would never have had an interest in God or the Lord Jesus. I was just lying there wondering what the point was of this trip, Uncle Fred and everything. I guess that was the only way God could get through to us. We have seen His promises fulfilled from the Bible, but what have we given in return? Nothing! Nothing at all!"

"I'm not sure I'm with you," Jerry replied, confused.

"We wouldn't have ever been too interested in your uncle or what he believed if we had not ended up on this adventure, right?" Linda explained excitedly. "We got to know him so well and he left his Bible in the boat, and because of that we've found out that his God is a real God and is interested in us. He's kept us safe when we left Jersey, on the sea and on the beach. Just now I realised what He wants. What God really wants is for us to trust His Son as our own Saviour just like Uncle Fred did in Belfast."

"How do we do that?" Jerry answered, becoming more interested in what Linda was saying.

"By obeying the verse we read in the boat," Linda replied. "You know the one where the Lord Jesus says 'I am the way'. He's the way to heaven. He also said something like 'No one comes to the father but by Me'. I realised just now that I can give myself to Him by believing on the Lord Jesus and understanding that He died on the cross to take my own sins away and make me fit for heaven. You know, Jerry, I have just trusted Him as my Saviour."

Jerry looked thoughtfully at his friend through tired eyes. "It's a bit too much to take in this late at night," he answered. "I haven't quite worked it all out for myself. I'll think about it more tomorrow after a good night's sleep."

"Oh, Jerry!" Linda said, disappointed. "I was hoping you would trust Him tonight too."

"I would," Jerry answered, "but it's too late for my brain to work tonight. You can tell me again tomorrow."

The next day the two soldiers knocked on the children's bedroom doors bright and early. "Wakey, wakey," Brian called out cheerfully. "It's breakfast time."

"What time is it?" said a sleepy voice from behind Linda's door.

"Eight," Cuthbert replied, "and breakfast is only served until nine so you need to get your skates on."

A door opened and Jerry's head appeared, topped with his thick brown mop of curly hair. Brian had removed the bandage and he now showed the scar he had received where the boat had struck him. "We didn't think to bring our skates with us," quipped Jerry cheekily.

"Get on with you," Brian teased back, pushing Jerry back into his room.

"Ouch!" said Jerry. "Mind my arm!"

"Sorry," apologised Brian, "but do hurry up or all the food will be gone."

"Have you thought anymore about what I said last night, Jerry?" Linda's voice called across the corridor.

"I was trying to work it out," Jerry called back. "I think I realise that God loves me and that the Lord Jesus died for me. How do I trust Him, like you did?"

Cuthbert and Brian, waiting in the corridor, looked at each other with expressions of amazement on their faces

Linda's door opened, and as her head popped out, she answered, "It's simply a matter of faith, Jerry. Simply accept what God has said about us being sinners and ask His Son to save you."

"I don't think I'm hearing right," Cuthbert said, turning to Brian. "Here are two children having a discussion about faith in God."

"Yes, I think it's a good thing. I wish I had thought about it more as a child," Brian commented.

"But how do I ask Him to save me?" Jerry called back, as he opened his door.

"I just got on my knees and prayed," Linda told him from across the corridor, oblivious of the two soldiers listening to them. "I asked Him when I realised that God must love me and that the Lord Jesus was the only way to heaven." Then after a pause she added, "And I told him that I was very sorry about my sin too!"

"Come on, we need to get breakfast!" Cuthbert called impatiently.

"Coming," called the children in unison.

The four of them entered a small dining room with neat tables each covered in a cheery red checked table cloth. Brian chose a table next to the window overlooking the courtyard where the taxi had dropped them off the previous evening. They all studied the menu which was chalked on a slate board. "What, no sausages?" exclaimed Brian, in dismay.

"There is a war on," Cuthbert reminded him.

They ordered their food and then Cuthbert explained the plans of the day. "Colonel Fleming phoned this morning. He asked if we would accompany you both to a family he has found for you to stay with in Berkshire."

"But we are not going to Berkshire," Jerry said firmly.

"We would like to go to Jersey," Linda added.

The two soldiers looked across at Jerry and Linda, and Cuthbert said, "We know that's what you want, but you can't just sail away from England and expect to land up in Jersey." Despite all their efforts both men realised that all their persuasion and arguing was not going to make the two youngsters change their minds.

Brian and Cuthbert looked at each other as Cuthbert tore off a piece of bread from a roll in his hand and leaned towards the two in a conspiratorial manner.

"Well, actually," Cuthbert pronounced with a grin on his face, "Brian and I were discussing this last night and we felt that we were the best people to help you get back home."

"Whoppee!" squealed Linda in jubilation, causing a few looks in her direction from nearby tables.

"Shush! Not so loud," scolded Brian as he leaned closer to the two children over the table. "We could both get court marshalled for this."

"Or shot!" suggested Cuthbert, with a comical expression on his face.

"What do you mean by court marshalled?" Jerry enquired seriously.

"Put on trial by the army for disobeying orders," Brian answered. "It's a serious thing. We could be put in prison and thrown out of the army. But we thought if we could persuade Colonel Fleming to get you housed with a family somewhere safe on the Isle of Wight instead of in Berkshire, you might have a much better chance to get safely away from there and across the Channel to home," Brian continued in a hushed tone. "We could keep an eye out and an ear to the ground for any possibility of a boat crossing the Channel. However, you must be really patient because it could take some time before we find a way of repatriating you and the war may be over before then." He paused, looked at the children and asked, "So what do you think?"

"What did you say you wanted to do with us?" Linda asked as a puzzled frown crossed her young face.

"Get you to stay in a home on the Isle of Wight," Cuthbert repeated.

"No, you said you wanted to re...re...er...re something to us," Linda quickly replied.

"Oh," said Brian, "repatriate you. It means get you back home!"

"Oh yes, yes, yes!" Linda answered almost triumphantly. "I want to be repatriated. That's another thing I was praying about last night."

"Well," interrupted Jerry as he stood up from the table, "before I get repatriated I think I need to get right with God. You're right, Linda, God has done so much for us and I have been so ungrateful. I'm off to my bedroom to sort this out once and for all."

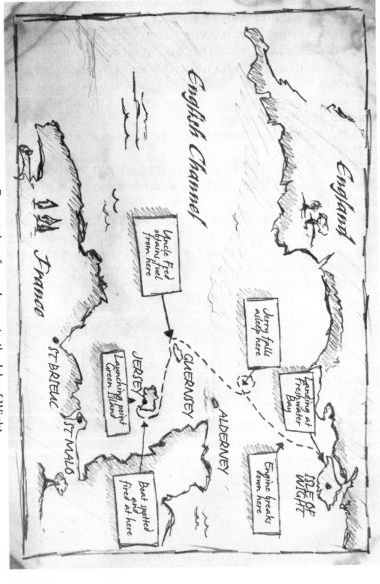

Route taken from Jersey to the Isle of Wight